SPANISH

for the

REST OF US

WILLIAM C. HARVEY, MS

1 2 3 4 5 6 7 8 9 LWI 26 25 24 23 22 21

ISBN   978-1-260-47326-1
MHID   1-260-47326-0

e-ISBN   978-1-260-47327-8
e-MHID   1-260-47327-9

Language Lab App

Extensive audio recordings (requiring Internet connection) and vocabulary flashcards are available to support your study of this book. Go to www. mhlanguagelab.com to access the online version of this application, or to locate links to the free mobile app for iOS and Android devices. More details about the features of the app appear on the inside front and back covers.

Contents

How to Use This Book

This book includes helpful features (marking boxes and sidebars) that each have a unique purpose.

QUICK TIPS: These boxes generally list additional insights and/or details about the section's primary theme. They also explain more difficult concepts and often provide examples.

MESSAGES: These texts, sent to you by author team Bill and Cecilia, announce, command, or "post" urgent things to always keep in mind.

CHOOSE 'n' USE!

CHOOSE 'n' USE! These boxes are for on-your-own practice, containing 5 or 6 open-ended sentences, with no answers provided.

¿PUEDE RECORDARLO?
(Can You Remember It?)

¿PUEDE RECORDARLO? These appear at the end of each chapter. Again, they are open-ended comprehension questions related to what has just been presented.

BillTalks

¡Yo hablo español!
Check the app for an introduction from your author, Bill.

¡YO HABLO ESPAÑOL! These are more than 80 references to audio practice podcasts (BillTalks), direct from your author, Bill. See the inside cover for details on how to connect online or via app. Listen and repeat along with the audio feature.

Hola, Fellow English Speakers!

Not everyone can take a Spanish course and learn something. So, finally, after years of teaching classroom Spanish using the dreadful "textbook approach," I got fed up and decided to try something different.

Having picked up Spanish myself by hanging around non-English speakers, I'd discovered what people *really* needed to speak *español*. So, with the help of my Spanish-speaking friend Cecilia, I put together a series of practical, easy-to-follow shortcuts, tips, and secrets to success – designed specifically for folks who aren't interested in "studying" a foreign language.

In place of traditional units and lessons, **Spanish for the Rest of Us** is intended as a guidebook and offers nothing more than helpful suggestions. This approach should make your language learning experience easy and *muy divertida* (lots of fun)!

Adiós for now,
Bill and Cecilia

BillTalks

1

¡Yo hablo español! Check the app for an introduction from your author, Bill.

Reasons Why Spanish Is Easy to Learn

Learning other languages is great, but believe me, I've chosen Spanish because it is the easiest of them all! I've spent a lifetime developing **Spanish for the Rest of Us** for six very good reasons.

1   Spanish is a lot like English.
Most Spanish words have the same Latin-based form as their English equivalents. Many words in both languages look and sound almost the same, which makes guessing a breeze.

2   Spanish is not complicated.
Conversations in Spanish can be kept short and sweet. Complex messages are often exchanged using only a few simple words. Only an understanding of basic grammar and pronunciation patterns is needed for successful communication to take place.

3   It's okay if you blow it.
Spanish speakers worldwide enjoy helping English speakers who try. Hispanics are generally proud, warm-hearted people who admire those with a sincere interest in learning their native tongue. So cheer up. Lousy Spanish only makes *you* feel stupid.

4   Spanish is not hard to practice.
All around the world, the Hispanic population continues to grow at a tremendous rate. Thanks to the Internet, regular exposure to Spanish should not be a major problem. Neither should it be difficult for the learner to find someone to "practice with." Also remember that in addition to Spain, lots of Spanish still lies just south of the US border.

5 Spanish can be profitable.

American business people have discovered that buying and selling in more than one language makes good business sense. And with Hispanics globally now spending hundreds of millions a day, their market has become a primary target of businesses everywhere. Increasingly, companies are providing Spanish training for their employees. And better pay seems to make learning that much easier. So revise that "résumé" Learning Spanish can lead to greater financial success!

6 Spanish is fun to learn.

There's nothing like the thrill of speaking Spanish and being understood for the first time, or even the second time. It won't be long before you'll get "hooked." Maybe that's because communication in a new language allows you to meet, understand, and assist more people, which does wonders for the self-image. Spanish also can make life more fun! Besides traveling to Spanish-speaking countries, in many parts of the USA, common activities such as shopping and dining out suddenly become more enjoyable and exciting. A second language is like a new toy – so play with it! After mastering Spanish you will find that similar languages, like French, Portuguese, and Italian, are easier to learn. And don't worry about staying motivated. It seems that once you get rolling in *español*, you're usually very difficult to stop!

BillTalks

¡Yo hablo español! Check the app for more on busting common myths about language learning.

Who Needs This Book?

This book is not for everyone.

For those of you who plan on living in Spain or Latin America and need extensive language training, I'm sorry. And to those who already speak Spanish and are looking to improve their reading and writing skills, I apologize.

You see, this guidebook was not written for people whose intentions are to "study" or work extra hard at language lessons.

This Book Is for the Rest of Us

Most of what you'll find here is basic, practical information that you can use right away, with a lot of the technical "stuff" trimmed away. Generalizations about Spanish are made, and translations are not "precise."

The primary theme is to assist folks who struggle with foreign languages, as they begin communication with Spanish speakers at work, while traveling, or at play.

Before You Begin

Okay, brace yourselves! This guidebook contains no drills, no worksheets, and no tests!

Instead, learners will be asked to follow some
RATHER UNUSUAL GUIDELINES

A   Forget what you've been told! (You'll just get hung-up on useless details.) There's no such thing as perfect Spanish, so don't get stuck trying to figure out the best way to say something. This book gives you only what you need to know. Instead of traditional grammar and pronunciation practice, try the practical shortcuts, tips, and secrets to successful communication. If you follow the useful suggestions, you'll be all right most of the time.

B   Spend most of your time listening! (You'll be talking in no time.) To learn the way a baby learns language, it's important to "take in" lots of Spanish at the beginning. Listen to fluent speakers. Soon, new words will emerge naturally in everyday conversation. Use the one-liners and greetings freely, but don't force speech until you feel ready to speak. Online language programs, mobile apps, and interactive devices can be helpful. But real-life practice is better!

C   Act as if you know more than you do! (You'll soon believe that you are fluent.) Learn to have self-confidence around people who speak only Spanish. Even if you don't understand a word, smile and laugh a lot. "Concentrate" when you are asked a question, and always answer with a short response. Imitate verbal and nonverbal expressions. Be assertive, but remain friendly. Experiment with new words and phrases. Fake it, and you'll be speaking Spanish ***pronto***!

D Don't make excuses! (You'll never get started if you do.) Thanks to modern research, we now know that the following statements about language learning are **Untrue**!

> You need to do grammar exercises......................*¡No!*
> You need to develop good pronunciation...........*¡No!*
> You need to start at an early age........................*¡No!*
> You need to memorize vocabulary lists.................*¡No!*
> You need to be "good at languages" ....*¡No!*
> So there! The truth is you have *no excuse* and . . .
> You *will* learn Spanish quickly and easily............*¡Sí!*

E Most of all, relax! The idea of learning a new language scares the life out of most people; so don't feel ashamed. Just accept the fact that you're going to sound strange and look awkward for a while. It's no big deal. This guidebook is designed to relieve you of stress and frustration. Never give up! Don't worry about a thing, have some fun, and just go for it. With **Spanish for the Rest of Us**, learning *no es problema*.

The Checklist

1 **Comfortable chair** ❏
2 **Background music** ❏
3 **Favorite beverage** ❏
4 **Laid-back attitude** ❏

1

CHAPTER *UNO*
¿Habla español?
(Do You Speak Spanish?)

Spanish Words the Rest of Us Already Know

americano	*cerveza*
amigo	*margarita*
amor	*tequila*
español	*vino*
loco	*bueno*
macho	*grande*
padre	*mucho*
rodeo	*más*
pueblo	*guacamole*
rancho	*adiós*
señor	*gracias*
señorita	*feliz Navidad*
Los Ángeles	*cucaracha*
fiesta	*por favor*
cha-cha-cha	*pronto*
tango	*sí*
olé	*dinero*
quesadilla	*uno*
burrito	*dos*
chile	*tres*
enchilada	*salsa*
taco	*problema*
latino	*hombre*
chiquita	*bravo*

Care to add a few more?

_____

_____

_____

Spanglish

A unique blend of Spanish and English has gradually evolved worldwide as more and more Spanish speakers and English speakers have made attempts to communicate. Something called "*Spanglish*" is alive and well (though words may vary from region to region). You see, many English words either can't be exactly translated into Spanish or are just easier to say when mixed with English. What's great is that they all sound similar to words the rest of us know. Check out this list of easy-to-remember "**Spanish English-isms**":

BillTalks

¡Yo hablo español! Check the app for more on Spanglish.

SPANGLISH	ENGLISH	SPANISH
rentar	to rent	*alquilar*
cachar	to catch	*atrapar*
puchar	to push	*empujar*
grocear	to go grocery shopping	*ir de compras*
cuitiar	to quit	*renunciar*
lonchar	to have lunch	*almorzar*
parquear	to park	*estacionar or aparcar*
taipiar	to type	*escribir a máquina*
wachar	to watch	*mirar*
textear	to text	*mandar texto*

QUICK TIPS

If it's close, they'll probably get it! Since Spanglish and English are so similar, you really don't need to worry about pronunciation.

Spanglish is not street slang! But it's not Spanish, either. So some people may make comments. Be prepared!

Did you know: Mixing both languages when you can't remember a word is still okay!

Más Spanglish Words

la baika	bike	*la bicicleta*
las brekas	brakes	*los frenos*
la carpeta	carpet	*la alfombra*
la marketa	market	*el mercado*
el mofle	muffler	*el silenciador*
el pay	pie	*el pastel*
el raite	ride	*el paseo*
la troca	truck	*el camión*
la yarda	yard	*el jardín*

 **QUICK TIP**

Are you aware that names of people, cities, streets, buildings, companies, and brand names are not usually translated into Spanish?

el Hilton

los Pampers

los Levis

el Kleenex

la Budweiser

Disneyworld

 Don't struggle with the pronunciation of Spanish words yet! You'll be getting the "Secrets to Sound-making" shortly.

Vamos a Chicago.	Let's go to Chicago.
El señor Rubio habla español.	Mr. Rubio speaks Spanish.
Trabajo en el Marriott.	I work at the Marriott.

The same is true for many acronyms and abbreviations: *CNN, NBA, AT&T,* etc.

Understanding Spanish Speakers

¿Holaamigocómoestá?

You're right. It does sound like one long word. Everything is just too fast. So what are you supposed to do? Well, don't panic. Relax, take a deep breath, smile, and try **Five Secrets to Success:**

1 Focus on the message.
Listen for key words and how they're expressed, instead of trying to understand the whole *enchilada*. Are they asking or telling you something? Focus on the tone of their voice. Avoid translating each word. Concentrate on the main idea only.

2 Use your hands and face.
Express comprehension by pointing, moving, or touching things. Make faces. Write or draw what you think they're trying to say. Use your phone! Be as expressive as you can. Soon, they'll get into the act. Don't give up, and you'll eventually end up communicating *sin* (without) *problemas.*

3 Say: *Más despacio, por favor.* (Mahs dehs-pah'-see-oh, pohr fah-bohr')
That means: "More slowly please." Or say *¿Qué?* (keh) or *¿Cómo?* (koh'-moh) which mean "What?" and "How's that?" Let them know you'd like to hear what they said again!

4 Listen for the English.
Since both languages are Latin based, many Spanish words sound a lot like English. Guess, and you'll probably be right!

5 Relax and try again.
Swallow your pride and remember – they're having as much trouble as you are. Lighten up, keep it fun, believe in yourself, and *español* will begin to make sense.

BillTalks
4 *¡Yo hablo español!* Check the app for more on steps to understanding Spanish.

¡Oye, escucha!
(Hey, listen!)

Don't say a word! You don't have to. Much like children learn their native tongue, it's best to listen first! So don't force yourself to speak. After listening to Spanish for a while, it will gradually start coming out of you! For now, try some of these easy (and inexpensive) ways to pick up on those new "foreign noises":

• Listen to Spanish radio stations (check local listings).
• Find out which TV stations also air in Spanish.
• Watch Spanish movies (with English subtitles).
• Search for Spanish downloads, podcasts, and video clips.
• Ride city buses or subways through Spanish-speaking areas.
• See a Spanish language play or musical performance.
• Attend a Spanish-speaking religious service of your faith.
• Join a Spanish-speaking club, team, or organization.
• Check into travel packages to Spain or Latin America.
• Befriend those Spanish speakers whom you see regularly.
• Take a Spanish class, or buy a program with lots of online practice.
• Download a Spanish learning app.
• Shop or dine at places where Spanish is spoken all around you.
• Keep going, and try to be creative!

You can obviously add your own ideas to this list. But however you choose to *escuchar* (listen), always remember the three Cs: **C**alm down, Observe **C**losely, and **C**oncentrate on what's being said!

The Non-Verbals!

Guess what? If you'd like to communicate in Spanish, but don't feel like speaking, there's an easy and fun way to send messages. As with most cultures, certain hand signals, facial expressions, eye contact, and body language convey valuable meaning. Here are some of my favorite hand signals that happen to be from Mexico.

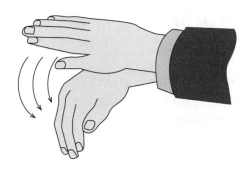

Venga
Come here.

By moving your hand (or arm) in a downward motion, you're calling someone to come toward you.

Un momento.
Just a moment.

By putting your thumb and index finger together, you're telling someone, "Hold on just a moment. I'll be right with you."

No, gracias.
No thanks.

By moving your pointer finger back and forth, you're telling someone "No" or "Don't."

¡Ojo!
Beware!

Pointing to your eye means "Be careful!" or "Watch out!"

¡Qué grande!
How big!

Always point upwards, with palm side of the hand towards you, when referring to the height of a person; and outwards, palm side down, when referring to the height of an object or animals.

Practice the non-verbals and you'll be able to communicate right away!

If you know how to say the words, add them for emphasis! There are many more "non-verbal signals" based on where folks are from, so take time to observe people as they interact. Ask the meanings if you're not sure.

I love it! Talk without speaking!

¿PUEDE RECORDARLO?
(Can You Remember It?)

I know we have just begun, but why not stop and review a moment before moving on to the next chapter. Just answer as many questions as you can, and don't worry about looking up the answers. It's all up to you!

- ☑ Give at least two reasons why Spanish is easy to learn.
- ☑ What are some of the guidelines to learn Spanish quickly?
- ☑ Name five Spanish words you knew before reading this book.
- ☑ What is *Spanglish?*
- ☑ How can you get folks to slow down when they are speaking Spanish very fast?
- ☑ List two activities that can help you practice listening to Spanish.
- ☑ Give a "hand signal" in Spanish.

2

CHAPTER *DOS*
Las primeras palabras
(The First Words)

The Secrets to Sound-making

Basically, you need to know **only five primary Spanish sounds** (the vowels) that will make you comprehensible and help you to understand more. When speaking Spanish, if you make the following sounds every time the corresponding letter appears, you'll sound just like a native speaker. When? Every time the letter appears! Try making these sounds toward the front of your mouth – instead of the back - with little or no air coming out. Short, choppy sounds are better than long, stretched-out ones. Go ahead, practice now that nobody's listening and soon you will be able to impress your friends!

 **QUICK TIP**

Exactness doesn't matter! As I said before, if it's close, they'll probably get it. Besides, the goal of this guidebook is getting people to communicate, not teaching all the different Spanish sounds. So stop fretting. You sound great to me!

Trust me! Know these and you'll be on your way!

a (ah)   like yacht

e (eh)   like met

i (ee)   like keep

o (oh)   like so

u (oo)   like spoon

The Big Five

a   *banana, cucaracha, cha-cha-cha, mañana*

e   *tres, excelente, olé, elefante, Pepe*

i   *sí, dividir, Trini, Miami, Lidia*

o   *loco, ocho, no, Colorado, dos*

u   *Lulú, mucho, tu, burro, Uruguay*

BillTalks

¡Yo hablo español! Check the app for more on the Big Five vowels.

Las "otras" (The "Others")

The "Big Five" was easy, but what about the "other" sounds in Spanish, such as the consonants? Good news – they're not much different from English. But here are a few that may cause confusion.

c and ***g***

c has two sounds: ***c*** like cat and ***c*** like celery, when followed by ***e*** or ***i***.

g also has two sounds: ***g*** (g) like go and ***g*** (h) like hello when followed by ***e*** or ***i***.

h	(Don't pronounce it; like the k in knife.)		
j (h)	like hot	***qu*** (k)	like kiss
ll (y)	like yes	***v*** (b)	like break
ñ (ny)	like canyon	***z*** (s)	like sit

Like the vowels, these consonant sounds have no exceptions! In Spanish, respective sounds are always the same every time their corresponding letter appears. Now, let's try to put all these "pieces of noise" together. Refer back to the "Secrets to Sound-making" as you read the following (ALOUD):

BillTalks

¡Yo hablo español! Check the app for more on consonants to practice.

c #1	*coco, carro, Colorado, capitán*
c #2	*Cecilia, cigarro, centro, cilantro*
g #1	*gorila, garaje, guacamole, Paraguay*
g #2	*general, Geraldo, gimnasio, rígido*
h	*huevo, hombre, hola, ahora*
j	*Juan, trabajo, frijoles, Julio*
ll	*llama, millón, tortillas, amarillo*
ñ	*señor, mañana, español, piña colada*
qu	*poquito, qué pasa, tequila, quesadilla*
v	*vino, Victoria, viva, hasta la vista*
z	*López, cerveza, Venezuela, González*

QUICK TIPS

- These 8 are the only "toughies." The rest can be pronounced the same as English!
- Take note! The rest of us have the most trouble with ***qu***.

> More volume!
> I can't hear you!

Easy as *UNO, DOS, TRES*

Don't worry about your "regional accent." Making yourself understood in Spanish doesn't depend on what part of the United States or English-speaking world you are from.

UNO   Always try to "visualize" Spanish words because they're spelled exactly as you say them. And don't worry about what you sound like!

DOS   Run the words together! What's really nice about the *español* is that it's put together in little pieces – much like the *inglés*. So, to sound like a native speaker, *thefasterthebetter!*

TRES   Read 'em right! By now, you've probably noticed the little accent mark (´) on parts of certain words. Don't get nervous. It only means that you're supposed to say that part of the word LOUDER! *Ma-rí-a* (Mah-REE-ah). Speaking of accent marks, as for the little words, like *sí* or *qué*, that's just how they're spelled!

SOUND	ENGLISH	PRACTICE WORDS	
que	keh	*pequeño*	*porque*
qui	kee	*chiquito*	*quiero*
ji or gi	hee	*jinete*	*gigante*
je or ge	heh	*jefe*	*general*
gue	ghe	*juguete*	*guerra*
gui	ghee	*guitarra*	*seguir*
ce	seh	*celebrar*	*cebolla*
ci	see	*cine*	*cilantro*
lle	yeh	*lleno*	*calle*
lli	yee	*gallina*	*pollito*
lla	yah	*llama*	*silla*
llo	yoh	*bello*	*llorar*
llu	yoo	*lluvia*	*velludo*

QUICK TIP

• Here's a great way to practice some of your new Spanish sounds: simply read each practice word aloud, and look up their meanings in English later on.

Más Pronunciation Details!

• If there's no accent mark, say the last part of the word louder (*español* = ehs-pahn-YOHL).

• For words ending in a vowel, *n* or *s*, the second to the last part of the word is emphasized (*taco* = TAH-koh).

• With *rr*, roll your R's – but only if you can. They'll understand if you use *r* instead.

• The *d* sometimes sounds like our "th" (as in "this") in the middle and at the end of words. Try it: *nada*, *todo*, *adiós*, *libertad*.

• People from Spanish-speaking countries don't all sound alike, but they all understand one another and will usually understand you.

• Forget all the pronunciation "rules." They'll only make it worse. Just try!

• Check out the **"Ten Talking Tips" for The Rest Of Us** on page 211.

• Once you become familiar with the different Spanish sounds, you'll make the first giant step toward fluency! So why not go back and read the section on "Sound-making" again!

You won't find any more pronunciation "guides" next to words in this book. Instead, learn the "Secrets to Sound-making" and practice in "real-life" situations!

Spanish Words That Don't Need Translating

There are literally thousands of Spanish words that are easy to understand. All you have to do is focus on the English within. No need to translate these:

Easy

aplicación	*favorito*	*operación*
arte	*fotografía*	*persona*
béisbol	*importancia*	*policía*
café	*inteligente*	*posesión*
cámara	*interesante*	*posible*
comercial	*limón*	*refrigerador*
conversación	*mapa*	*teléfono*
escuela	*millonario*	*televisión*
especial	*minuto*	*turismo*
estúpido	*momento*	*universidad*
familia	*nervioso*	*vacación*
fantástico	*noviembre*	*vocabulario*

The Easiest

banana	*golf*	*natural*
chocolate	*horrible*	*rodeo*
color	*hospital*	*popular*
doctor	*hotel*	*radio*
final	*idea*	*taxi*
digital	*simple*	*terror*

Other Easy *palabras* to Remember

diccionario	*instrumento*
dieta	*moderno*
dólar	*música*
eléctrico	*producto*
elegante	*profesional*
información	*sexo*
programa	*presidente*
reservación	*sincero*
violento	*restaurante*

Start today! Make a *lista* of Spanish words (without looking back) that you have already "picked up." You'll be surprised!

Go ahead – read everything aloud!

QUICK TIPS

- Remember: No pain – no gain! As in all stretching exercises, when you pronounce this stuff, make it hurt! Use those "mouth muscles"!
- Spanish sounds a bit like English – but with an accent!
- Be careful! Some Spanish words look like *inglés*, but aren't. For example, *contestar* (to answer) has nothing to do with contests. And *pan* (bread) or *pie* (foot) could cause confusion, too!
- "Add" an upside-down mark in front of all exclamations and questions:

  Do you understand?
  ¿Comprende usted?

  Yes! I understand!
  ¡Sí! ¡Yo comprendo!

Speak up!
(¡Hable!)

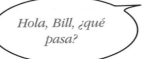

Hola, Bill, ¿qué pasa?

Yo, er . . . mumble . . . mumble . . . mumble

More Ways to *practicar*

Speak up! There's no need to stress about "sounding dumb." All that matters is that you somehow manage to understand each other.

Listening to Spanish was no big deal. The next step, then, is to practice saying something. Once you've warmed up with Spanish words that resemble English, try these practice techniques for improving pronunciation, while picking up the hard-to-remember stuff:

- Next time you're at a Hispanic restaurant, order food for everyone at the table.

- Travel through Spanish-speaking sections of town and say aloud the words on billboards and store windows. (You may get funny looks!)

- Randomly download materials on the Southwest, Latin America, or Spain, and try pronouncing all the Spanish words you find.

- Next time you're alone, try reading English aloud – but use the Spanish Secrets to Sound-making! Don't laugh – it works!

- Start slowly. Try practicing one sound a week!

- Record yourself regularly while reading Spanish language articles, stories, or other reading material.

- If possible, buy some language apps and work with them.

- Get on the Internet and search for a Spanish-speaking chat room or blog. Find out all the ways to interact online with your Spanish-speaking friends.

- Again, there is nothing better than speaking face to face with a Spanish-speaker. Are you willing to try?

QUICK TIP

The best way to learn a new language is to talk face to face with someone. Think of convenient ways to learn Spanish from Hispanic people. One popular method is to offer a little English instruction in return.

Baby's First *Palabras* (Words)

We've taken a look at words the rest of us already know and should know. Now it's time to try words and phrases you have to know. In the same way a baby learns "survival words" at first, it's best to start with the Spanish that will take you the farthest. The following seem to be the words acquired first in any language. Use them to communicate complete messages. (Wait! Check back on the Secrets to Sound-making!)

BillTalks

¡Yo hablo español! Check the app for more on baby's first *palabras*.

adiós	goodbye	*hombre*	man
agua	water	*más*	more
amigo	friend	*mucho*	a lot
baño	bathroom	*mujer*	woman
bueno	good	*muy bien*	very well
carro	car	*niño*	child
casa	house	*nombre*	name
celular	cell phone	*número*	number
comida	food	*persona*	person
dinero	money	*por favor*	please
gracias	thanks	*ropa*	clothing
grande	big	*trabajo*	work
hola	hi		

So how's your sound-making?

My Favorite First Words

Here are more gems that work all by themselves.

algo	something	*alguien*	someone
ahorita	right now	*los demás*	the rest of them
después	afterwards	*ninguno*	none of them
antes	before	*cualquiera*	any of them
mientras	during	*cada uno*	each one
entonces	then	*ambos*	both of them
ya	already	*algunos*	some
demasiado	too much	*varios*	several
otra	another or other	*nada*	nothing
		siguiente	the next one
otra vez	again	*mismo*	the same
casi	almost	*diferente*	different
juntos	together	*primero*	first
solo	alone or only	*último*	last
todo	all of it	*en todas partes*	everywhere
nadie	no one		

The Greetings and Stuff

Having any problems in getting started? Your troubles are over. Memorize these as one long word and they'll think you're fluent!

¡Hola! ¿Qué tal?	Hi! How's it going?
Buenos días.	Good morning.
Buenas tardes.	Good afternoon.
Buenas noches.	Good evening or Good night.
¡Adiós!	Bye!

Más cortesías (More Courtesies)

"Hello?"

¿Aló?, ¿Bueno? or *¿Diga?* are all good when you answer the phone. "Who's calling?" is *¿De parte de quién?*

"Who's there?"

When you knock and want to enter, it's *¿Se puede?* (Can I come in?). To say "Come in!" use *¡Pase!* or *¡Adelante!*

"Thanks!"

Instead of the old, *Muchas gracias* for "Thanks a lot," try these stronger words of appreciation: *¡Muchísimas gracias!* (Thanks so much!) *¡Mil gracias!* (Thanks a ton!) or the one I use: *¡Muy amable!* (You're so kind!)

Por favor is "Please."
De nada is "You're welcome."
Lo siento is 'I'm sorry."

BillTalks
8 *¡Yo hablo español!* Check the app for more on greetings.

BillTalks
9 *¡Yo hablo español!* Check the app for more on survival one-liners.

BillTalks
10 *¡Yo hablo español!* Check the app for more on questions.

"Excuse me!"

Whenever you'd like to get through a crowd, use *¡Con permiso!* If you cough or sneeze, say: *¡Perdón!* To get someone's attention, try saying *¡Disculpe!* "Go ahead" is *¡Pase!* and "Bless you!" is *¡Salud!.* Keep in mind that having good manners is very important in building new relationships!

¿Qué pasa? vs. *¿Cómo está usted?*

This is the standard "What's happening?" Sometimes you'll be greeted with *¿Qué . . .* (and something else). Don't worry! They're still only asking what's going on. Here's the easy way out: always answer with *¡Sin novedad!* or *¡Nada!* (Nothing new!)

Everyone knows this one. It means, "How are you?" And as with *¿Qué pasa?,* when you hear, *¿Cómo_____?* (How "something"?) you can sneak by using the classic, *¡Muy bien!* (Just fine!)

QUICK TIPS

- *¿Y usted?* means, "And you?"
- *¿Qué pasó?* is "What's the matter?" or "What happened?"
- And mind your manners!

Later on, we'll take a look at other ways to answer these *¿Qué . . . ?* and *¿Cómo . . . ?* questions.

Remember that Spanish speakers exchange greetings regularly. Try learning other ways folks say hello, and don't be afraid to "greet" someone back!

Las presentaciones (Introductions)

BillTalks
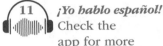
11 *¡Yo hablo español!*
Check the
app for more
on greetings
in everyday
conversation.

- There are many ways to say "Nice to meet you!", but the most common is *¡Mucho gusto!* During the introduction, don't forget to shake the other person's hand. If something is said to you first, smile and say *¡Igualmente!*, which translates to, "Same to you."
- *¿Cómo se llama?* (What's your name?) and *Me llamo* _____ (My name is _____) are also nice to know!
- Even if you make a mistake, smiling always leaves a good impression!

¿Dónde está? (Where is it?)

Watch and listen for *está*! See if you can guess how it's used.

More than likely, one of the first questions you'll get asked will be "Where's the _____?" (Whenever anyone needs directions, they'll use, *¿Dónde está . . .?*) Here, then, is what you'll need:

. . . *a la derecha* = to the right

. . . *a la izquierda* = to the left

. . . *adelante* or *derecho* or *recto* = straight ahead

. . . *aquí* or *acá* = here

. . . *allí* or *ahí* = there

. . . *allá* = over there

¡Viva el vocabulario!
(Long Live Vocabulary!)

Following are three groups of words most folks seem to pick up and use almost immediately.

Los números (The Numbers)

0	**cero**	5	**cinco**
1	**uno**	6	**seis**
2	**dos**	7	**siete**
3	**tres**	8	**ocho**
4	**cuatro**	9	**nueve**

BillTalks
¡Yo hablo español! Check the app for more on the low numbers.

Los colores (The Colors)

black		*negro*
blue		*azul*
brown		*café*
gray		*gris*
green		*verde*
orange		*anaranjado*
purple		*morado*
red		*rojo*
white		*blanco*
yellow		*amarillo*

BillTalks
¡Yo hablo español! Check the app for more on colors.

Fill in the circles with colored pencils or markers to help memorize the colors.

BillTalks

¡Yo hablo español! Check the app for more on common objects.

La clase (The Class)

BillTalks

¡Yo hablo español! Check the app for combining common objects with command words.

el libro

la mesa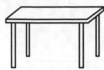

el lápiz

la pantalla

la pluma

la carpeta

el papel

el escritorio

el cuaderno

la silla

la pizarra

el cesto de basura

CHOOSE 'n' USE!

Here are some sentences that will help you put these words to practice. Fill in the blanks, read each sentence aloud, and plan ways to use them in real-life situations.

Los números

Mi número de celular es . . .	My cell number is . . . (615-778-8934, etc.)
¿Dónde está el cuarto número . . .?	Where's room number . . . (five, three, etc.)?
Necesito. . . más.	I need . . . (10, 20, etc.) more.

Los colores

Me gusta el color . . .	I like the color . . . (purple, red, etc.).
¿Es . . . o . . .?	Is it . . . (black, etc.) or . . . (white, etc.)?
Hay algunos de color . . .	There are some . . . (orange, etc.) ones.

La clase

¿Tiene un/una . . .?	Does it have a . . . (wastebasket, whiteboard, etc.)?
. . . está en . . .	The . . . (paper, pen, etc.) is "in," "on," or "at" the . . . (desk, table, etc.)
Traiga . . .	Bring the . . . (folder, book, etc.)

At the end of this book you'll discover a **Personal Success Chart**. Use it! Simply pencil in your "experiences." Try out your new skills regularly. See how fast your *lista* can grow!

Learn all the things in the classroom today!

la tableta (tablet) *la computadora* (computer)
la impresora (printer) *la pizarra inteligente* (smart board)
el proyector (projector)

QUICK TIPS

- More numbers will be introduced later. Can you say the preceding numbers with your eyes closed?
- Look up more colors if you need others. And learn by "word-picture association." For example, BLANK white paper is *blanco*. (How clever can you be?)
- More new words are on their way. For now, go find these things around you. Touch them and name them in *español* – and no cheating!

¿PUEDE RECORDARLO?
(Can You Remember It?)

☑ Pronounce the five vowels in Spanish (The Big Five!).

☑ Write three Spanish words that are spelled the same in English.

☑ Name one way you plan to practice "speaking" Spanish.

☑ Give one expression in Spanish that is used to greet someone.

☑ Say the numbers 1 through 9 in Spanish.

3

CHAPTER *TRES*

Más, más, más

(More, More, More)

The *El* and *La* Business

If you want to name a single object or person, put either **el** (masculine) or **la** (feminine) in front. It may seem strange, but as you continue to learn more **español**, you will need to know the meanings of "masculine" and "feminine." In Spanish, single objects require either an **el** or a **la** in front. This has nothing to do with an object's sex (LOL)! It's just the **el** and **la** Business!

In order to remember which one to use, just check to see if the word ends in either an **o** (generally masculine) or an **a** (generally feminine). People are easy because males get **"el"** and females get **"la"**:

BillTalks

¡Yo hablo español! Check the app for more on **el** and **la**.

QUICK TIPS

- A few words are weird (i.e., **el sofá, la mano, el problema**).
- Many words don't end in **o** or **a** (i.e., **la paz, el elefante, el visor**) so you'll need to memorize them.
- **El** and **la** refer not only to male and female persons (i.e., **el señor, la dama**), but to animals as well.
- It doesn't matter if you get confused and use the wrong one, you'll still be understood! So don't hold back!

el

el taco
el amigo
el burro

la

la enchilada
la señorita
la cucaracha

More *El* and *La* Business – plus *Un* and *Una*

The following are common questions and answers about one part of Spanish that is completely foreign to English:

1 Can *el* and *la* also refer to more than one person, animal, or thing?

No way, *José*. Two or more **tacos** and **enchiladas** become: **los tacos** and **las enchiladas**.

Notice what happens with **el**. More than **uno** is **los**. See? You've got to tag on the "**s**" at the end.

2 How do I say "a" or "an" instead of "the"?

At times in English we use "a" or "an." To say "any old thing" in Spanish, use **un** or **una**: **un taco** and **una enchilada** are "a" **taco** and "an" **enchilada**.

3 Why is this aspect of Spanish a little confusing?

The answer is simple: You're not used to it yet! Grasping these concepts may take a little time. Besides, your messing up Spanish won't make much difference! Your listeners will figure out what you said anyway. But if you do "get corrected" just say to yourself: "I'll get it right the next time!"

And guess what? *Unos* and *unas* mean "some."

Words (naming things, people, or concepts) that have the following endings, usually need **la** (feminine) in front:

–a	la casa
–sión	la depresión
–tad	la libertad
–ción	la acción
–dad	la sociedad

QUICK TIPS

- By the way, *él* with an accent mark means "he."
- *Uno* is "one" also!
- Talking about "more than one" (plurals) is a lot like *inglés: cuatro tacos* (four tacos)

BillTalks

17   *¡Yo hablo español!* Check the app for a review of what you've learned so far.

The Once-and-for-All Rule

BillTalks

18

¡Yo hablo español! Check the app for more on the Once-and-for-All Rule.

Muchos means "many." *Mucho* means "a great deal" or "a lot." (And don't confuse *mucho* with *muy*, which means "very.") Here are other words that tell "quantity":
poco = a little bit
poquito = a very little bit
pocos = a few
poquitos = very few

As we've learned, talking about "more than one" (plural) in Spanish is very much as it is in English: *un taco < dos tacos*. Words not ending in a vowel take "*es*" at the end: *un doctor < dos doctores*.

What isn't like English is what I call the "Once-and-for-All Rule." You see, not only do all Spanish words that name (nouns) or describe (adjectives) things, people, or concepts need *s*, or *es* to make them plural, but when they are used together, the final *o*'s and *a*'s (masculine and feminine) must match:

Muchos tacos deliciosos   Many delicious tacos
y (and)
Muchas enchiladas
deliciosas   Many delicious enchiladas

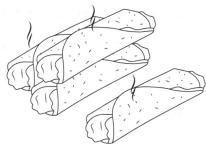

QUICK TIPS

- You can expect to get the hang of this *rápido.*
- Matching the *o*'s and *a*'s works great with "*los colores*": Many white cars = *Muchos carros blancos.*
- But watch out with words ending in some letters: Many blue cars = *Muchos carros azules.*

Did you notice -*ito* and -*ita* word endings reduce things?

The ONE-A-DAY One-liners

A very good way to gain confidence while learning a new language is to speak in short, meaningful phrases. Instead of struggling with the formation of correct long sentences, expressive one-liners can be used – especially when there's really nothing left to say. And using them will make you feel more confident! You'll sound more fluent than you actually are. Practice a new one every day . . . (Careful! They're addictive!)

Use these phrases whenever you think it might be appropriate:

BillTalks

19

¡Yo hablo español! Check the app for more on favorite expressions.

¡No es cierto!	That's not true!	*¡Me alegro!*	I'm so glad!
¡Buena idea!	Good idea!	*¡Ojalá!*	I hope so!
¡Claro!	Sure!	*¡Por supuesto!*	Of course!
¡Cómo no!	Why not!	*¡Quizás!*	Maybe!
¡Con razón!	No wonder!	*¡Sin duda!*	No doubt about it!
¡Creo que sí!	I think so!	*¡Tanto mejor!*	All the better!
¡De acuerdo!	I agree!	*¡Ya veo!*	I see!
¡Depende!	That depends!	*¡Yo también!*	Me, too!
¡Es posible!	It's possible!	*¡Yo tampoco!*	Me, neither!
¡Es verdad!	That's right!	*¿Así?*	Like this?
¡Lo que quieras!	Whatever you want!	*¿Está bien?*	Is that OK?
¡Más o menos!	More or less!	*¿Quién sabe?*	Who knows?

For Busy *personas*

¡Ya me voy!	I'm leaving now!
¡Ya se fue!	He or she has left!
¡Ahora vengo!	I'll be right back!
¡Ahí viene!	Here he or she comes!
¿Listo?	Ready?
¡Vamos!	Let's go!
Todavía no.	Not yet.
Ahora no.	Not now.
En punto.	On time.

⚡ QUICK TIPS

- Caution! Rudeness will ruin communication!
- These one-liners are great at *fiestas*. Here, for example, is a bit of one-liner dialogue:
  María: *¿Listo?* (Ready?)
  Carlos: *Creo que sí. ¿Y Tomás?* (I think so. And Thomas?)
  María: *¡Ahí viene!* (Here he comes!)
  Carlos: *¿Y Carolina?* (And Carolina?)
  María: *¡Ya se fue!* (She's left!)
  Carlos: *¡Está bien!* (Okay!)

¡Más One-liners!

No entiendo or *No comprendo.*	I don't understand.
No sé.	I don't know.
No me importa.	I don't care.
Muchas veces.	Many times.
A la vez.	At the same time.
Una vez.	Once.
Al revés.	Backwards.
Boca abajo.	Upside down.
Lo contrario.	The opposite.

BillTalks

20

¡Yo hablo español!
Check the app for more on personal comments.

These expressions are often used instead of *adiós*:

¡Vaya con Dios!	Go with God!
¡Chau!	Bye!
¡Cuídese!	Take care of yourself!

QUICK TIPS

- Try to remember each as one-long-word! (Use the Secrets to Sound-making!) And have fun!
- Embarrassed? Then go somewhere private to read aloud, and shut the door!

¡Salúdeme a su (mamá, papá, etc.)!	Say hi to your (mom, dad, etc.)!
¡Mi más sentido pésame!	Accept my condolences!
¡Dele un abrazo!	Give him/her a hug!
¡Buen viaje!	Have a nice trip!
¡Tenga buen día!	Have a good day!
¡Diviértase!	Have fun!
¡Que disfrute!	Have a good time!
¡Que le vaya bien!	Take care!
¡Que se alivie!	Get well!

Use these *expresiones*, but with *mucha emoción*:

¡Felicitaciones!	Congratulations!
¡Feliz Navidad!	Merry Christmas!
¡Feliz cumpleaños!	Happy Birthday!
¡Socorro!	Help!
¡Caramba!	Wow!
¡Dios mío!	For heaven's sake!
¡Mentiras!	Lies!
¡Silencio!	Quiet!
¡Basta!	Enough!
¡Vaya!	Go on!
¡Buena suerte!	Good luck!
¡Salud!	Cheers! or Bless you!

QUICK TIPS

- To learn even more one-liners, listen carefully and ask Spanish speakers what words and phrases mean.
- Repeat and practice until you feel prepared. Write your favorite phrases as a note on your cell phone, but be sure to memorize the sounds!

Keep Talking!

*Es muy*_____.	It's very_____.	*¡Qué*_____	
cierto	certain	*asco!*	How disgusting!
correcto	correct	*barbaridad!*	How awful!
difícil	difficult	*bueno!*	How great!
fantástico	fantastic	*chiste!*	What a joke!
importante	important	*importa!*	So what!
interesante	interesting	*lástima!*	What a shame!
necesario	necessary	*locura!*	How crazy!
obvio	obvious	*raro!*	How strange!
terrible	terrible	*rico!*	How tasty!
		ridículo!	How ridiculous!
		suerte!	What luck!
		tonto!	How dumb!
		triste!	How sad!
		va!	No way!

Time to Chat

If you've been paying attention, this won't be difficult. All you do is look at the picture and then try to figure out what would be the best "natural" response in Spanish. Speak up, and write it only if you want to. Go ahead and use any of the words and phrases introduced so far:

Try more than one response. Check any previous page for possible responses. And, just as you would do in an actual situation – be natural and creative!

Fantastic *frases*

For the bravest of babblers, here are some "advanced plays" that truly make folks sound like they know what they're talking about:

A propósito . . .	By the way . . .	*Por ejemplo* . . .	For example . . .
Además . . .	Besides . . .	*Por eso* . . .	Therefore . . .
Al principio . . .	At first . . .	*Por fin* . . .	At last . . .
En cuanto a . . .	Regarding . . .	*Por lo menos* . . .	At least . . .
En general . . .	In general . . .	*Según* . . .	According to . . .
O sea . . .	In other words . . .	*Sin embargo* . . .	However . . .
Paso a paso . . .	Step by step . . .	*Sobra decir* . . .	Needless to say . . .
Poco a poco . . .	Little by little . . .	*Sobre todo* . . .	Above all . . .

Here are examples of how it's done.

¿Mi carro? En general, mi carro es excelente.	My car? In general, my car is great.
Por ejemplo, el color es perfecto.	For example, the color is perfect.
Además, es muy grande.	Besides, it's very big.
Sin embargo, el motor no es bueno.	However, the engine isn't any good.
¿Mi carro? No sé.	My car? I don't know.

Now, you try some:

_____

_____

_____

I Have a *Pregunta*! (Question)

Suggestions for Success

Try to apply the following suggestions when making questions and giving answers in Spanish:

- Focus on the first word! There are only a few "question words," so learn them. The next step is to listen for main words in the question that you can recognize or "guess at." Concentrate on the "topic" of conversation.

- Answer as briefly as possible! Take your time. And if you want, repeat the question you've been asked. At first, only respond with key words and short phrases.

- Relax and remember your English! Whether you're asking or answering, try using each word just as you would in English. Again, it's OK to mix both languages if you should forget!

The Primary *Preguntas en español*

Make **muy** sure you can both understand and say the life-saving **pregunta** words that follow:

¿ ? ? ¿ ?

¿Cuál?	What/Which?
¿Cómo?	How?
¿Qué?	What?
¿Dónde?	Where?
¿Cuánto?	How much?
¿Cuántos?	How many?
¿Quién?	Who?
¿Cuándo?	When?

BillTalks
21
¡Yo hablo español! Check the app for more on **cuál** questions.

¿Cuál?

Let's begin with the **cuál** questions, which can sometimes be answered with one or two words. Here are the most common ones needed to get basic information. Notice how **¿Cuál es su . . .?** means "What is your . . .?"

¿Cuál es su nombre?	What's your name?	**Mi nombre es Juan.**
¿Cuál es su dirección?	What's your address?	**Mi dirección es 363 Main St.**
¿Cuál es su número de teléfono?	What's your phone number?	**Mi número es (888) 555-1234.**
¿Cuál es su lugar de nacimiento?	What's your place of birth?	**Mi lugar de nacimiento es Cuba.**
¿Cuál es su correo electrónico?	What's your email?	**Mi correo electrónico es Bill@Spanish.com**

¿Cuál es su libro?	Which (one) is your book?
¿Cuál es su lápiz?	Which (one) is your pencil?
¿Cuál es su cuaderno?	Which (one) is your notebook?

¿Cuál? all by itself usually means "Which one?" **¿Cuáles?** is the word for "which" when there are more than one: **¿Cuáles son sus amigos?** (Which <u>ones</u> are your friends?).

¿Cómo?

BillTalks

¡Yo hablo español!
Check the app for
more on Spanish
names.

Keep in mind the following when you ask for a person's
name.

¿Cómo se llama? is another popular way to ask, "What's
your name?"

> *Primer nombre* is "first name."
>
> *Apellido* is "last name."
>
> *Me llamo . . .* is "My name is . . ."

BillTalks

¡Yo hablo español!
Check the app for
more on *qué* and
cómo questions.

Juan   José
Primer nombre
(Not all Hispanic people have two first names!)

López
Apellido paterno
(Dad's last name)

Pérez
Apellido materno
(Mom's last name)

QUICK TIPS

- All the *pregunta*
  words need accent
  marks. A few change
  meaning when you
  drop the accent:
  como (I eat) and *que*
  (that).
- Always put a "¿" at
  the beginning of a
  question, as well as
  the "?" at the end.
  (¿Está bien?)
- Slow down, relax! Ask
  your questions and
  give your answers:
  palabra por palabra
  (word by word),
  letra por letra (letter
  by letter),
  número por número
  (number by number).
- "*su*" means "his,"
  "her," "their," or "its"
  in addition to "your."
  So you may need to
  "point!"

–In the United States, this guy
is just *Juan López*.
–Traditionally, when a woman marries,
she keeps her dad's last name,
followed by her husband's.
–There's no "middle name"
as we know it.

All alone *¿Cómo?* means "What?" or "How's that?" Use it like
"How?"

The classic *¿Cómo se llama?* literally means "How are you
called?"

Now, can you tackle these other *cómo* concepts?

¿Cómo se dice?	How do you say it?
¿Cómo se escribe?	How do you write it?
¿Cómo está?	How are you?

¿Qué?

¡Qué . . .! with exclamation marks means, "How . . .!" as in *¡Qué inteligente!* (How intelligent!).
¿Qué? always means "What?" as in *¿Qué pasa?* (What's happening?). Here are more *qué* questions.
Picture a scenario and ask:

¿Qué pasó?	What's the matter?
¿Qué es esto?	What's this?
¿Qué es eso?	What's that?
¿Qué son?	What are they?
¿Qué significa?	What does it mean?
¿Qué hora es?	What time is it?
¿Qué hay de nuevo?	What's new?

BillTalks
24

¡Yo hablo español! Check the app for even more on *qué* and *cómo* questions.

¿Dónde?

¿Dónde? is for directions; it is the "Where?" word. Whether you're looking for a person, place, or thing, just fill in the blank:

¿Dónde está _____?   Where's _____?

"Look for" these phrases also:

¿Dónde vive?	Where do you live?
¿Dónde trabaja?	Where do you work?
¿Adónde/Dónde va?	Where are you going?
¿De dónde es?	Where are you from?

BillTalks
25, 26

¡Yo hablo español! Check the app for more on *dónde* questions.

Check the app for answers to *dónde* questions. For more location words, see page 144.

¿Cuánto? vs. ¿Cuántos?

¿Cuánto (a)? is the shopping word.	*¿Cuántos (as)?* is often used for counting.
Cuántos applies to masculine nouns.	*¿Cuántos amigos?*
Cuántas applies to feminine nouns.	*¿Cuántas amigas?*

BillTalks
27

¡Yo hablo español! Check the app for more on "the shopping words."

BillTalks
28, 29

¡Yo hablo español! Check the app for more on *quién* questions.

Check the app for review of the question words you've learned so far.

You can always "count" on these phrases:

¿Cuántos años tiene?	How old are you?
¿Cuántos hay?	How many are there?
¿Cuánto tiempo?	How much time?
¿Cuánto cuesta?	How much does it cost?

Long responses to these questions sound strange, so avoid using complex sentences. Keep those answers short!

BillTalks

30

¡Yo hablo español! Check the app for more on the WHEN words in Spanish.

QUICK TIPS

- Words change a bit when you want to refer to past action. Don't be concerned! For now, use them as you would one-liners:
¿Cuándo fue?
When was it?
Fue _____.
It was _____.
¿Qué dijo?
What did he/she say?
Dijo _____.
He/She said _____.
¿Cuántos había?
How many were there?
Había _____.
There were _____.
- Caution! The word *mañana* = tomorrow, but *la mañana* = morning, so *mañana por la mañana* is tomorrow morning.

If you feel that you've had enough for now, take a break! Walk around, name things, or try out new words you've already learned. I'll be here when you return!

¿Quién?

¿Quién es?	Who is it?
¿Quiénes son?	Who are they?
¿Quién habla?	Who's speaking?
¿De quién?	From whom/Whose?
¿A quién?	To whom?
¿Con quién?	With whom?

¿Cuándo?

We'll be reading the clock and calendar soon, so let's warm up with some *¿Cuándo?* questions:

¿Cuándo . . .	When . . .
. . . empieza?	. . . does it begin?
. . . termina?	. . . does it end?
. . . llega?	. . . does it arrive?
. . . sale?	. . . does it leave?
. . . regresa?	. . . does it return?
¿Cuándo llega?	When does it/he/she arrive?
Hoy.	Today.
Mañana.	Tomorrow.
Por la mañana.	In the morning.
Por la tarde.	In the afternoon.
Por la noche.	At night.

Who's Who?
¿Quién es quién?

BillTalks

31

¡Yo hablo español! Check the app for more on personal pronouns.

Yo   I

Usted You (formal)

These *quién* words (subject pronouns) work wonderfully as one word responses. Notice how they also "start you off" when expressing a complete message:
¿Quién es inteligente? Ella es inteligente.
(Who is intelligent?)
(She is intelligent.)

Ella   She

Él   He

Ellos They

Ustedes   You guys

Nosotros   We

Obviously, **Ellas** = "They," feminine; **Nosotras** = "We," feminine.

QUICK TIPS

- You'll hear these words as well: *Tú* = "You," informal; *Vosotros* = "You guys" informal
- *Él, ella, ellos,* and *ellas* can refer to things as well as people: *Los libros, ¿dónde están ellos?* (The books, where are they?)
- "Grab onto" the *quién* words in all questions, because they will make answering so much easier!

The little word **tu** (your, informally) is also really common: **¿Cómo está tu madre?** (How's your mom?).

QUICK TIPS

Just add "**s**" to both words (possessive adjective and noun) when talking about more than one:

• **Son mis amigos.**
  <u>They're my friends.</u>

• **Son sus amigos.**
  _____

• **Son nuestros amigos.**
  _____

QUICK TIP

The word **de** also means "from."
Here's the formula:
    From him
    De él
    El dinero es de él.
    From them
    De ellos, ellas
    _____
    From us
    De nosotros
    _____

BillTalks

32 **¡Yo hablo español!** Check the app for more on **de quién** questions.

Posesión (Words that Show Possession)

mi *amigo*
(my friend)

su *amigo*
(their, your, his, or her friend)

nuestro *amigo*
(our friend)

¿De quién es? (Whose is it?)

If someone (or something) "belongs to" someone else, use **de** (of) to tell "who" the person or thing belongs to. Notice the reverse word order:

It's Maria's friend.   ***Es el amigo de María.***

It's Juan's apartment.   ***Es el apartamento de Juan.***

The *Posesión* Principles

• Don't forget the **El** and **La** Business, so that the endings "match": ***nuestra amiga*** (our friend).

• Don't get possessive words (adjectives) mixed up with the **quién** words (pronouns):
  <u>**Yo** tengo **mi** carro.</u>   I have my car.

• Try these possessive words once in a while:
  Es (It's) . . .   **mío**   mine.

                   suyo   yours, his, hers, or theirs.

- When you get stuck, always escape with *de*: *¿Es Paco un amigo de . . .* (Is Paco a friend of . . .)

BillTalks
33   *¡Yo hablo español!* Check the app for more on possession.

usted?	yours?
él?	his?
ella?	hers?
ellos?	theirs (masculine)?
ellas?	theirs (feminine)?
ustedes?	yours, you guys?
nosotros?	ours?

- Perhaps you haven't noticed, but sometimes *en español,* it's OK to drop the *quién* word! It's already understood who's involved: (*Yo estoy bien* or *Estoy bien* both mean "I'm fine").

- "Casual" or informal Spanish is centered on the little word *tú* (not to be confused with "tu", which means "your" in an informal setting). *Tú* means "you," same as *usted*, However, while *usted* is used to address anybody with respect, *tú* is the "you" used with children, your family, or friends. Here's an example: *Tú estás en tu casa.* (You are at your house.)

QUICK TIPS

Who knows? You may come across these words once in a while. Practice the pattern, without being concerned about the grammar:

myself	*yo mismo*
I do it myself.	*Lo hago yo mismo.*
yourself	*usted mismo*
himself	*él mismo*
herself	*ella misma*
yourselves	*ustedes mismos*
themselves	*ellos mismos*
ourselves	*nosotros mismos*

The Reversal Rule

BillTalks

¡Yo hablo español!
Check the app
for more on the
Reversal Rule.

In speaking Spanish, it is sometimes necessary to think backwards! For example, if you'd like to describe something, just reverse the order of the describing word (adjective) and that of what's being described (noun):

A lot of good tacos
Mu<u>chos</u> ta<u>cos</u> buen<u>os</u>

When you talk, try to recall the **Once-and-for-All Rule** and the *El* and *La* Business (feminine and masculine gender). But don't let this slow you down. Forgetting sometimes won't hurt anything!

You'll probably encounter ***muchos ejemplos más*** (many more examples), but fear not – you'll catch on!

This "REVERSING" is everywhere!

- Use it for possession:
  It's John's house.
  Es la casa de Juan.

- As well as for giving addresses:
  Where is 642 Broadway Avenue?
  ¿Dónde está la Avenida Broadway 642?

- In addition, some sentences are actually "reversed":
  I like coffee.
  El café me gusta.

- And so are many "one-liners":
  Not now!
  ¡Ahora no!

¡ENTREVISTA! INTERVIEW!

If you're truly serious about learning **español**, the **entrevista** is for you. Here's how it works: Simply "prepare" three common questions and then write one in each top box to the right of the words **Los nombres** (names). See chart below. Next, go some place nearby where you can easily "interview" Spanish speakers. List their names under **Los nombres**. (To get their names, use Question #1.) Fill in their responses in the boxes to the right under each question:

Los nombres (Names)	¿Cuál es su nombre? (What's your name?)	¿Cómo está usted? (How are you?)	¿De dónde es usted? (Where are you from?)
José López	José	Bien	Puerto Rico
Marta Sánchez			
Luis Pérez			

Now, grab a clipboard or your phone and head to places where you can practice:

- An "authentic" Hispanic restaurant.
- A family gathering or party.
- A Hispanic foods market.
- An English as a Second Language (ESL) class.
- A Hispanic cultural celebration, festival, or holiday event.
- Almost any Spanish speaker in the world is more than willing to "chat" with you online!

Información (Info)

- The more you learn, the more "complex" your questions will become. No need to "force it" now.

- Spend time "chatting" with folks throughout the interview. It's fun!

- Start slowly. Practice first with people you feel more comfortable with.

- A three-question interview like this takes less than 2 minutes per person. "Too busy" is no excuse!

- If you should have trouble understanding, just have folks "write-in" their own responses!

The *Superpreguntas*

The following are *más* than just survival questions – they're *super*!

Before moving forward, can you quickly translate these "*pregunta*" words into English?

¿Cómo?	_____
¿Dónde?	_____
¿Qué?	_____
¿Cuántos?	_____
¿Cuánto?	_____
¿Quién?	_____
¿Cuándo?	_____
¿Le gusta?	Do you* like it?
¿Entiende?	Do you* understand?
¿Quisiera?	Would you/he/she like it?
¿Hay?	Is/Are there any?
¿Por qué?	Why? (By the way, *Porque*, without the accent and spacing, is "Because")

¿Quiere?	Do you* want it/some/to?
¿Tiene?	Do you* have it/some?
¿Puede?	Can you/he/she do it?

*Also: *Does he* or *Does she.*

These ***superpreguntas*** are powerful only when other words are added. Take a chance and toss in words you already know:

¿Le gusta . . .? (Do you like . . .?) **la fiesta, el taco, el color,** etc.

¿Entiende usted . . .? (Do you understand . . .?) **el inglés, el problema, el libro,** etc.

¿Quisiera usted . . .? (Would you like . . .?) **agua, cerveza, café,** etc.

¿Hay muchos . . .? (Are there a lot of . . .?) **hombres, burritos, animales,** etc.

¿Por qué no está en . . .? (Why aren't you in . . .?) **la casa, Chicago, el carro,** etc.

¿Quiere usted más . . .? (Do you want more . . .?) **salsa, dinero, amigos,** etc.

¿Tiene usted . . .? (Do you have . . .?) **un tractor, una idea, mucho vocabulario,** etc.

QUICK TIP

Question words are also used as "relative pronouns" in Spanish, too (but without the accent mark):
Es el hombre que me gusta. (He's the man that I like.)
Es Carlos, del cual se oye tanto. (It's Carlos, about whom you hear so much.)

 Once you "get" that first word, next try focusing on exactly what it is they are asking you!

¿PUEDE RECORDARLO?
(Can You Remember It?)

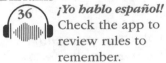

BillTalks

36

¡Yo hablo español!
Check the app to
review rules to
remember.

☑ Briefly answer these questions in Spanish (or English, if
you have to!):

¿Cuál es su número de teléfono?

¿Dónde vive usted?

¿Cuántos años tiene usted?

¿Quién es su amigo (o amiga)?

¿Cómo se dice en español? (Just fill in the translations!):

last name   *apellido*

address   _____

today   _____

tomorrow _____

when   _____

what   _____

4

CHAPTER *CUATRO*

Mucho más

(Much More)

49

Do You Know Your A-B-C's? (*El alfabeto*)

A
B
C

Once you get rolling, you'll find yourself asking people everywhere how to say things *en español*. At work, in public, or on the phone – learning words will simply be part of your everyday routine. Remember the following *frases*? Well, go ahead and use them to "pry."

¿Qué es esto?	What's this?
¿Cómo se dice?	How do you say it?
¿Qué significa?	What does it mean?

They're *muy importantes*, yet sometimes you'll have to ask folks to "write it for you." Here are two lines that may help:

¿Cómo se escribe?	How do you write it?
¿Cómo se deletrea?	How do you spell it?

Simply hand them a pen and ask for it: *Letra por letra, por favor.* (Letter by letter, please.)

El alfabeto

BillTalks

37 *¡Yo hablo español!* Check the app for more on spelling with the Spanish alphabet.

1   You already know the Big Five – *a, e, i, o, u* – their names are just as they sound!

2   These other letters are "close" to English. Say them in both languages – now!

b	(beh "*larga*" or "*grande*")	*c*	(seh)
		d	(deh)
v	(veh "*corta*" or "*chica*")	*f*	('eh-feh)
		b	('ah-cheh)

k (kah)

l ('eh-leh)

m ('eh-meh)

n ('eh-neh)

p (peh)

q (coo)

r ('eh-reh)

s ('eh-seh)

t (teh)

w (veh 'doh-bleh)

x ('eh-kees)

3 Here are four Spanish letters that the rest of us have problems with:

g (heh) *j* ('ho-tah) *y* (ee-gree-'eh-gah) *z* ('seh-tah)

4 The ***alfabeto*** also has four more "letters" than ours. In order to pronounce them correctly, three are spelled with two letters together. And, one has a ~ on top!

ch (cheh) *ll* ('eh-yeh) *rr* ('eh-rreh) *ñ* ('en-yeh)

5 ***Muy bien***. Are you ready to read the ***alfabeto*** in order? I've added the "double letters," so go slowly – (one letter at a time!)

a, b, c, ch, d, e, f, g, h, i, j, k, l, ll, m, n, ñ, o, p, q, r, rr, s, t, u, v, w, x, y, z.

QUICK TIPS

- Spell everything aloud in Spanish from now on!
- But first, learn to spell your ***nombre*** and other ***información de emergencia*** (emergency information).
- Practice spelling over the ***teléfono***!
- Use your online ***diccionario*** or ***aplicación*** often! And practice saying words aloud when looking them up.
- Try teaching words ***en inglés*** to a Spanish-speaking person. You'll be forced to spell!
- As you learned from the **Secrets to Sound-making**, being "pretty good" is good enough!
- FYI: *"ll"* and *"ch"* have been cut from the official Spanish alphabet. However, people do refer to them when spelling out a word.

Folks sometimes refer to *el alfabeto* as *el abecedario*.

Take a *Número*

0-1-2-3-4-5-6-7-8-9

Sure, ***los números del 1 al 10*** are easy. But do you realize how valuable they really are? In certain emergencies, private, or very personal matters, just by stating one digit at a time, you can save yourself ***muchos problemas!***

¿Cuál es su . . .?

. . . ***número de teléfono*** (phone number) _____

_____

. . . ***número de seguro social*** (social security number)

_____

. . . ***número de licencia de conducir*** (driver's license number) _____

. . . ***domicilio*** or ***dirección*** (address) _____

. . . ***código postal*** (zip code) _____

. . . ***código de área*** (area code) _____

. . . ***código de acceso*** (pass code) _____

. . . ***número de apartamento*** (apartment number) _____

_____

. . . ***número de placa*** (license plate number) _____

_____

. . . ***número de tarjeta de crédito*** (credit card number)

_____

. . . ***número de celular***   (cell phone number) _____

_____

. . . ***número de cuenta***   (account number) _____

_____

If you don't know these numbers, go back to ***"¡Viva el vocabulario!"*** (page 23).

Don't write in sensitive personal information here – use fake numbers instead!

You get the idea. Daily, practice saying aloud everything from counting your pocket change to channels on the TV remote. Remember that the trick is to keep it easy – and fun!

Take Some *Más números*

Let's break down the rest of **los números** just as we did the Spanish **alfabeto** – it helps the memory. Use your own word-association system, and stay motivated by thinking of new ways you can use to practice every day!

1st First, some weird numbers:

10 **diez** (dee-ehs')

11 **once** (ohn'-seh)

2nd Next, the easiest of all:

12 **doce** (doh'-seh) Hear the "**dos**"?

13 **trece** (treh'-seh) Hear the "**tres**"?

3rd Now, try to pronounce these the best you can:

14 **catorce** (cah-tohr'-seh) Pronounced a lot like **cut-or-say**

15 **quince** (keen'-seh) Pronounced a lot like **king-say**

4th And how about some math?

(10) **diez y seis** (6) = (16) **dieciséis**

diez y siete = (17) **diecisiete**

diez y ocho = (18) **dieciocho**

diez y nueve = (19) **diecinueve**

5th 20 **veinte** (veh-een'-teh) is different because it ends in **-nte**, while these multiples of 10 all end in **-nta**. Listen for the smaller number inside:

30	**treinta** (treh-een'-tah)	**tres**
40	**cuarenta** (kwah-rehn'tah)	**cuatro**
50	**cincuenta** (seen-kwehn'-tah)	**cinco**
60	**sesenta** (seh-sehn'-tah)	**seis**
70	**setenta** (seh-tehn'-tah)	**siete**
80	**ochenta** (oh-chehn'-tah)	**ocho**
90	**noventa** (noh-behn'-tah)	**nueve**

BillTalks

38

¡Yo hablo español! Check the app for more on larger numbers.

BillTalks

¡Yo hablo español!
Check the app for more on really big numbers.

⚡ QUICK TIPS

• These are called the "ordinal" numbers:
1st *primera/o (María es la primera. Juan no es el primero.)*
2nd *segunda/o*
3rd *tercera/o*
4th *cuarta/o*
5th *quinta/o*
6th *sexta/o*
7th *séptima/o*
8th *octava/o*
9th *novena/ o*
10th *décima/o*

• By the way, *primero* and *tercero* lose their final letter when placed in front of masculine singular words:
Mi primer carro.
(My first car.)
Está en el tercer grado.
(He is in third grade.)

In Spanish, check out the difference in the numerical form of the ordinals:
1st = *1.°* 2nd = *2.°*
3rd = *3.°* . . . and so on.

6th   The numbers between are more math problems. Notice the spelling changes:

(20) *veinte y uno* (1)	=	(21) *veintiuno*
veinte y dos	=	(22) *veintidós*
veinte y tres	=	(23) *veintitrés*
_____	=	_____
_____	=	_____

7th   Keep counting!

100 is *cien* (see-ehn') (like "century").

101 is *ciento uno*.

201 is *doscientos uno* . . . etc.

8th   These "hundreds" are the only strange ones:

500 = *quinientos*

700 = *setecientos*

900 = *novecientos*

9th   And the simplest of all:

1.000 is *mil* (like "millenium").

2.000 is *dos mil*, etc.

(Note that periods, not commas, are used for thousands.)

10th   Now, let's put them all together:

3.562 = *Tres mil, quinientos, sesenta y dos*

8.974 = _____

16.100 = _____

Instant Time-Telling

Learning to tell someone what time it is in Spanish will take no time at all! Although there are other optional ways to do it, this is clearly the easiest and fastest way to go:

¿Qué hora es? (What time is it?)

Ready to respond? First, listen for **hora** which means the **hour** or **time**. To answer, just look at your **reloj** (a watch or clock) and give the **hora** followed by the **minutos**. Careful! There is no "o'clock" in Spanish:

> ***Son las . . .*** (It's . . .)
> **6:00** *seis*
> **6:20** *seis y veinte*

Other Timely Tidbits

. . .in the morning   ***de la mañana (AM)***   It's 6 AM = ***Son las seis y veinte de la mañana.***

. . .in the afternoon   ***de la tarde (PM)***
It's 4 PM = _____

. . .in the evening, at night   ***de la noche (PM)***
It's 10 PM = _____

Be ready! Some people will say things like:

a quarter past	2:15 = ***dos y cuarto***
10 minutes before	1:50 = ***dos menos diez***
half past	2:30 = ***dos y media***
at noon	***al mediodía***
midnight	***a la medianoche***
on the dot	***en punto***
minutes	***minutos***
seconds	***segundos***

¿Qué hora tienes? means the same thing!

BillTalks

¡Yo hablo español! Check the app for more on giving the time.

⚡ **QUICK TIPS**

- If it's 1:00–1:59 then use, *Es la . . .* instead of *Son las*: 1:40 = *Es la una y cuarenta.*
- If you want to say "At (a certain time)," say *A las . . .* At 6:05 = *A las seis y cinco.*
- *La hora* refers to "clock time," but *tiempo* means "time, in general."
- To tell time . . . notice you only need to know *1-59*!
- Have Spanish speakers teach you different ways to tell time!

Like other parts of the world, you may hear folks using "military clock time" instead!

International Dateline

Still another practical use of **los números** is the yearly calendar. Let's begin with the most common words and phrases having to do with **el calendario** (the calendar):

> No capital letters for days or months, **por favor**!

el día	the day
el mes	the month
la semana	the week
el fin de semana	the weekend
el año	the year

los días de la semana

el lunes	Monday
el martes	Tuesday
el miércoles	Wednesday
el jueves	Thursday
el viernes	Friday
el sábado	Saturday
el domingo	Sunday

BillTalks
41
¡Yo hablo español!
Check the app for more on days of the week.

los meses del año

1 **enero**	5 **mayo**	9 **septiembre**
2 **febrero**	6 **junio**	10 **octubre**
3 **marzo**	7 **julio**	11 **noviembre**
4 **abril**	8 **agosto**	12 **diciembre**

BillTalks
42
¡Yo hablo español!
Check the app for more on months of the year.

Be sure to review any other words you've heard before:

today	**hoy**
tomorrow	**mañana**
yesterday	**ayer**
next week	**la próxima semana**
last month	**el mes pasado**
the day before yesterday	**anteayer**
the day after tomorrow	**pasado mañana**
two days ago	**hace dos días**

¿Cuál es la fecha? (What's the date?)

The year is always read as one large number:

2022 = *dos mil (2000) veintidós (22)*

And whenever you give the date, apply the "Reversal Rule":

June 3rd = *el tres de junio*

You try:
April 15th _____
August 20th _____
January 1st _____

CHOOSE 'n' USE!

Los días

Hay una fiesta . . .	There's a party . . . (on Saturday, on Friday, etc.)
¿Trabaja usted . . .?	Do you work . . .? (on Monday, etc.)
El programa empieza . . .	The program begins . . . (on Thursday, etc.)

Los meses

Ayer fue el _____ de _____.	Yesterday was the (20th, etc.) of . . . (August, etc.)
Mi cumpleaños es en . . .	My birthday is in . . . (February, etc.)
¿Tiene usted vacaciones en . . .?	Do you have vacation in . . .? (October, etc.)

Calendario Express!

Besides the basic calendar words, it's nice to have other key words and expressions that will help get any date-line message across. As always, practice these aloud first, before you actually "go for it"!

QUICK TIPS

- Ask "*calendario*" questions with *¿Qué? ¿Cuál?* or *¿Cuántos?*
- Look! January (*enero*) is the only month that doesn't look like *inglés*!
- Don't use ordinal numbers! Dates take cardinal numbers: 2 (*dos*), 3 (*tres*), etc. (Except for the 1st . . . It's *el primero de: el primero de agosto* or *el 1° de agosto*.)
- To say "in July," it's *en julio*. But, "on Monday" is *el lunes*, and "on Mondays" is *los lunes*. Notice no "on."
- "Vacation" is *las vacaciones*. To say "holiday," try *día feriado*.

To master these Spanish words, set a reminder alarm to say the time, day, and date at least once a day!

Say something! Respond briefly to the *"¿Qué día?"* questions right now:

¿Qué día es hoy?	What day is today?
¿Qué día es mañana?	What day is tomorrow?
¿Qué día fue ayer?	What day was yesterday?
¿Qué día fue anteayer?	What day was the day before yesterday?
¿Qué día es pasado mañana?	What day is the day after tomorrow?

¡Las estaciones! (The seasons!)

la primavera	spring
el otoño	fall
el verano	summer
el invierno	winter

¿Cuál es su estación favorita? Which is your favorite season? _____

¡Más palabras importantes en el calendario!

QUICK TIP

- *Hay* ("there is" or "there are") is a *muy* useful calendar word: *¡Hay una reunión mañana!*
- It's wise to learn full expressions, too, such as: *Tengo que hacer un mandado* (I have to run an errand.)

el próximo	the next one	*Vamos a Disneylandia el próximo verano.*
el pasado	the past one	
actual	current	
ahora	nowadays	
diario	daily	
mi horario	my schedule	
el aniversario	anniversary	*Mi aniversario es mañana.*
el cumpleaños	birthday	
el evento	event	
el mandado	errand	
el partido	game (sports)	
la cita	appointment	
la clase	class	
la fiesta	party	
la reunión	meeting	

¿Qué tiempo hace?
(How's the Weather?)

Making conversation with "weather chit-chat" is a must in any language and **¿Qué tiempo hace?** is a question that's **excelente** as an "ice-breaker." Then, you're bound to need these:

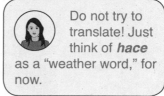

Do not try to translate! Just think of **hace** as a "weather word," for now.

Hace . . .	**It's . . .**
frío	cold
calor	hot
buen tiempo	nice weather

Está____.	**It's____.**
despejado	clear
lloviendo	raining
lloviznando	drizzling
nevando	snowing
nublado	cloudy
soleado	sunny
ventoso	windy

⚡ QUICK TIPS

- Here's the easy way!
  Hay . . .   There is
  or There are . . .
neblina	fog
granizo	hail
lluvia	rain
nieve	snow
humo	smoke
fuego	fire
- *Calor* ("hot" for weather) is not *caliente* ("hot" to the touch).
- *El clima* also means "the climate."

Más Weather Words

el agua	water	*el corrimiento de tierras*	landslide
el aire	air	*la inundación*	flood
el cielo	sky	*el huracán*	hurricane
los grados	degrees	*el relámpago*	lightning
el hielo	ice	*el terremoto*	earthquake
la marea	tide	*la tormenta*	storm
las nubes	clouds	*el tornado*	tornado
		el trueno	thunder

If the weather is not moderate, use:

¡Hace mucho calor!	It's very hot!
¡Hace mucho frío!	It's very cold!
Nieva mucho.	It snows a lot.
Llueve mucho.	It rains a lot.
Hace mal tiempo.	It's bad weather.

¿PUEDE RECORDARLO?
(Can You Remember It?)

☑ Count to one hundred by tens in Spanish.

☑ Give your birthdate in Spanish.

☑ In Spanish, tell what the weather is like today.

☑ Translate into Spanish: What time is it? What's the date? What's this? What's your address? It's snowing.

☑ Translate into English:

¿Cuál es su código de área?

Hay doce meses en un año.

¿Cuáles son los días de la semana?

¿Trabaja usted mañana?

La fiesta es hoy.

Hace mucho calor en el verano.

BillTalks

43

¡Yo hablo español! Check the app for some language activities to test what you've learned.

5

CHAPTER *CINCO*

Las personas

(People)

Es vs. está
(Is vs. Is)

Are you totally confused about the uses of *es* and *está*?

I say *es!*

And I say *está!*

STOP THE FIGHT!
They're both right.

When talking about yourself, *Estoy* and *Soy* can be used without the *Yo!*

In Spanish, to say "is" or "you are" . . .
. . . use *está* when referring to:

Location	*¿Dónde está Carlos?*	*Carlos está en la casa.*
Condition	*¿Cómo está Lupe?*	*Lupe está muy bien.*

. . . but, use *es* to indicate:

Qualities	*¿Marta es mejicana?*	*No, Marta es cubana.*
Characteristics	*¿Usted es inteligente?*	*Sí, pero ¡usted es más inteligente!*

Notice the difference. ***Está*** sounds more temporary, while ***Es*** sounds more permanent:

BillTalks

¡Yo hablo español! Check the app for more on *está* and *es*.

Está

Ella está nerviosa.	She is nervous.
La silla no está en el baño.	The chair is not in the bathroom.
Pedro está trabajando.	Pedro is working.

Es

El programa es importante.	The program is important.
Susana es profesora.	Susana is a professor.
¿Es usted puertorriqueña?	Are you Puerto Rican?

That's all you get for now! All this stuff is further explained in Chapter ***Siete***.

QUICK TIP

Está is one form of the verb ***estar*** and ***Es*** is a form of the verb ***ser***. Both verbs mean "to be." Look closely at these other forms, but don't try to memorize them now! (See pp 156–161 for more!)

First, try the forms of "***Estar***":

> *Yo* <u>*estoy*</u> *aquí y* <u>*estoy*</u> *contento.*
> I am here and I am happy.
> *Ellos* <u>*están*</u> *aquí y* <u>*están*</u> *contentos.*
> They are here and they're happy.
> *Nosotros* <u>*estamos*</u> *aquí y* <u>*estamos*</u> *contentos.*
> We are here and we are happy.

Got it? All the forms of the verb ***Estar*** are used to indicate current "condition" or "location"!

Now try ***Ser***:

> *Yo* <u>*soy*</u> *italiano.*
> I am Italian.
> *Ustedes* <u>*son*</u> *altos.*
> You guys are tall.
> *Nosotros* <u>*somos*</u> *actores.*
> We're actors.

See? All the forms of ***Ser*** are used to indicate more permanent "qualities" or "characteristics"!

Get It Together – Part I

It's time to begin linking your **palabras** together! Strings of words bound by logic create meaningful messages. And remembering that pronunciation and grammar have little effect on communication allows us to babble away more freely. Another helpful trick to recall is that words can be joined in much the same order in Spanish as they are in **inglés**!

When we speak, single words and one-liners are the easiest ways to communicate our ideas:

¡Sí!	Yes!
Es un amigo.	He's a friend.

And adding more words "to clarify" is not difficult:

¿Roberto? Sí, él es mi amigo.	Roberto? Yes, he is my friend.

Now, remember to use the "little linking words": **y** (and), **o** (or), and **pero** (but):

Él es mi amigo y ella es mi amiga, pero ella es más inteligente!
He's my friend and she's my friend, but she is more intelligent!

Put more words together. Do you remember any of this stuff?

El libro de Samuel . . .	Samuel's book . . .
. . . es azul y rojo,	. . . is blue and red,
. . . pero está en su casa.	. . . but, it's at his house.
¿Cómo se llama usted . . .	What's your name . . .
. . . y dónde vive?	. . . and where do you live?

En diciembre, hay nubes y hace mucho frío, y llueve mucho.
In December, it's cloudy and very cold, and it rains a lot.

BillTalks

45

¡Yo hablo español! Check the app for more on the linking words, **y**, **o**, and **pero**.

QUICK TIPS

- First, try **es** or **está**. Then, if your listener seems confused, smile and try it another way!
- In linking your Spanish words, recall and use these three concepts:
  1. The Reversal Rule
  2. The Once-and-for-All Rule
  3. The **El** and **La** Business

Never forget! Your Spanish pronunciation will improve the more you speak.

Still Confused About the Informal "*tú*" Form?

Some readers still might be wondering why I've continued to stress the "formal" **usted** form, and not the **tú** or so-called informal form of **es** and **está**. Think about it: it just becomes another thing the rest of us have to worry about! As you learned earlier, Spanish-speaking people use the intimate **tú** when speaking to their friends and family. But that's because they can understand each other! My point here is simple. By following these shortcuts and tips, soon, you too will be able to make friends and establish "informal" relationships with Spanish-speaking people. In no time your new pals will be teaching you the **tú** form, along with lots of other "inside info." Besides, the **usted** form is easier to remember and use. You'll find it's perfectly acceptable when speaking with anyone!

Here's what the **tú** form looks like:

¿Cómo estás <u>tú</u>?	How are you?
Es para <u>ti</u>.	It's for you.
Yo <u>te</u> quiero mucho.	I love you a lot.
<u>Tu</u> casa es bonita.	Your house is beautiful.
¿Es la <u>tuya</u>?	Is it yours?
¡Yo trabajo contigo!	I work with you!

 If you ever come across "***Ud.***" or "***Uds.***" in your Spanish reading, don't fret! They're abbreviations for ***Usted*** and ***Ustedes***.

How're You Doing?

We've talked already about the question *¿Cómo está usted?* (How are you?). And, we know that the answer *¡Muy bien!* (Very well!) is the old stand-by. Now let's check out the many other responses that tell folks how you feel.

If you want, talk about yourself!

Yo estoy _____.   I am (feeling) _____.

aburrido(a)	bored	*feliz, contento(a)*	happy
agotado(a)	exhausted	*fenomenal*	amazing
ansioso(a)	anxious	*fuerte*	strong
asustado(a)	scared	*mal*	not well
bien	well, fine	*más o menos*	not bad
cansado(a)	tired	*molesto(a)*	annoyed
confundido(a)	confused	*nervioso(a)*	nervous
débil	weak	*ocupado(a)*	busy
dormido(a)	sleepy	*orgulloso(a)*	proud
emocionado(a)	excited	*preocupado(a)*	worried
enfermo(a)	sick	*regular*	OK, alright
enojado(a)	angry	*sorprendido(a)*	surprised
fantástico(a)	fantastic	*triste*	sad

CHOOSE 'n' USE!

Estoy un poco . . .	I'm a little . . . (tired, sleepy, etc.).
¿Está usted muy . . .?	Are you very . . . (bored, anxious, etc.)?
Carolina está demasiado . . . y . . .	Carolina is too . . . (sad, etc.) and . . . (worried, etc.).
¿Cuándo está . . . usted?	When are you . . . (happy, etc.)?
¿Es una persona . . .?	Is he/she a . . . (busy, excited, etc.) person?

QUICK TIPS

- For emphasis, add:
  tan "so"
  ¡Estoy tan agotado!
  demasiado "too"
  un poco "a little"
  muy "very"
  más "more"
- Put two or three of these words together with *y* (and). *Estoy confundido y asustado.*
- Remember: *bueno* means "good," and *bien* means "well."
- You can also say *Yo soy* ____ instead of *Yo estoy* ____ if you want to talk about your personality and not your feelings.

 Using *Es* instead of *Está* can change the meaning of a message, so think before you speak:
Él es nervioso. He's a nervous person. (usually)
Él está nervioso. He is nervous. (now)

¡Qué cuerpo!
(What a Body!)

It's time to learn the Spanish names for different parts of the human body. After all, people are made **de carne y hueso** (of flesh and bone). To practice, either touch the picture below or your own body part! Follow this command: **Tóquese** . . . (Touch your . . .)

BillTalks

46

¡Yo hablo español! Check the app for more on parts of the body.

el pulgar
thumb

la cabeza
head

el dedo
finger

la muñeca
wrist

la mano
hand

el cuello
neck

el codo
elbow

el brazo
arm

el hombro
shoulder

el pecho
chest

la garganta
throat

el estómago
stomach

la espalda
back

la rodilla
knee

la pierna
leg

el tobillo
ankle

el dedo del pie
toe

el pie
foot

Más partes del cuerpo (More Body Parts)

la cadera	hip	*los músculos*	muscles
el cerebro	brain	*los nervios*	nerves
la cintura	waist	*el pelo, el cabello*	hair
el corazón	heart	*la piel*	skin
la costilla	rib	*los pulmones*	lungs
la espina dorsal	spine	*el riñón*	kidney
el hígado	liver	*la uña*	nail
las nalgas	buttocks		

  Keep touching!

La cara (The Face)

la barbilla	chin	*la mejilla*	cheek
la boca	mouth	*la nariz*	nose
las cejas	eyebrows	*el oído*	ear (inner)
los dientes	teeth	*el ojo*	eye
la frente	forehead	*la oreja*	ear (outer)
los labios	lips	*las pestañas*	eyelashes
la lengua	tongue		

¡Ayyy! (Ouch!)

Here are some Spanish words and phrases to help you express what may go wrong with the body. Create short sentences next to each one if you can:

nueve-uno-uno	9-1-1	*Llame al nueve-once*
el accidente	accident	*Es un accidente.*
la ambulancia	ambulance	*¿Dónde está la ambulancia?*

Other words for **el estómago** are: **la barriga** (belly) and **la panza** (tummy)

QUICK TIP

Learn as many emergency one-liners as possible. You never know!
Estoy muy mareado.
I'm very dizzy.
Tengo fiebre.
I have a fever.
Me duele el estómago.
My stomach hurts.
Hay dolor en la rodilla.
There's pain in the knee.
¡No puedo respirar!
I can't breathe!
¡Llame al doctor!
Call the doctor!

el análisis	test
la caída	fall
la contusión	bruise
la cortada	cut
la curita	bandaid
el derrame cerebral	stroke
el dolor	pain
la emergencia	emergency
la fiebre	fever
la herida	injury
el hueso quebrado	broken bone
el infarto	heart attack
la medicina	medicine
el médico	doctor
las muletas	crutches
la máscara	mask
los primeros auxilios	first aid
la sangre	blood
la silla de ruedas	wheelchair
el tratamiento	treatment
la vacuna	vaccine
el vendaje	bandage

Dolor de_____.

cabeza	headache
espalda	backache
estómago	stomachache
garganta	sore throat
muela	toothache
Me duele.	It hurts.

Me siento mejor.	I feel better.
Estoy malo(a).	I'm ill.
Estoy débil.	I'm weak.
Estoy mareado(a).	I'm dizzy.
Estoy resfriado.	I have a cold.

Familia Ties

Without a doubt, one of your initial encounters in Spanish will eventually lead to speaking about family members. But before we take a look at *la familia*, let's first make an effort to master these *muy importante* "people" *palabras*:

BillTalks
47
¡Yo hablo español!
Check the app
for more on
"people" words.

Try to say something about each one:

el hombre	man	*Tomás es un hombre muy inteligente.*
la mujer	woman	
el niño	small boy	
la niña	small girl	
el muchacho, el chico	young boy	
la muchacha, la chica	young girl	
el bebé	baby	
el adolescente	teenager	
el señor or Sr.	man or Mr.	
la señora or Sra.	lady or Mrs.	
la señorita or Srta.	young unmarried woman	
la persona	person	
el socio	business partner	
la pareja	relational partner	
el amigo	friend	
el mejor amigo	best friend	
el novio	boyfriend or groom	
la novia	girlfriend or bride	

el enemigo	enemy
el joven, la joven	young person
la persona mayor	older person
damas y caballeros	ladies and gentlemen
los amantes	lovers
los compañeros	buddies
los compañeros de cuarto	roommates

¡Más palabras referidas a personas!

alguien	someone
cualquier persona	anyone
mucha gente	a lot of people
nadie	no one
poca gente	a few people
todo el mundo	everyone

CHOOSE 'n' USE!

Lupe es . . .	Lupe is . . . (my little girl, my partner, etc.).
. . . está aquí.	The . . . (man, baby, etc.) is here.
¿Quién es . . .?	Who is the . . . (person, enemy, etc.)?
Tengo muchos . . .	I have lots of . . . (relatives, buddies, etc.).
No hay . . .	There aren't any . . . (boys, teenagers, etc.).
¿Dónde está su . . .?	Where is your . . . (boyfriend, bride, etc.)?

Los *padrinos* are "godparents." In most Spanish-speaking countries, the in-laws and godparents are considered important family members. Los *compadres* is the name parents and godparents of a child share.

Los miembros de la familia
(The Family Members)

Touch the following pictures with your finger. Read aloud and check for meanings!

Él es . . . (He is . . .) *Ella es . . .* (She is . . .) *. . . su . . .* (. . .his, her, your, or their . . .)

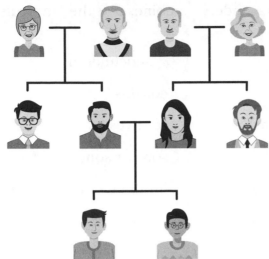

BillTalks

48

¡Yo hablo español!
Check the app for
more on using *su*
when discussing
your family.

Él es su esposo. *Ella es su esposa.*

Él es su padre. *Ella es su madre.*

Él es su hermano. *Ella es su hermana.*

Él es su hijo. *Ella es su hija.*

Él es su abuelo. *Ella es su abuela.*

Toda la familia

Grouping words in pairs always makes learning a lot simpler:

¿Quién es _____?	Who is (the) _____?		
el padre	father	*la madre*	mother
el hijo	son	*la hija*	daughter
el hermano	brother	*la hermana*	sister
el abuelo	grandfather	*la abuela*	grandmother
el tío	uncle	*la tía*	aunt
el esposo, el marido	husband	*la esposa*	wife
el suegro	father-in-law	*la suegra*	mother-in-law
el sobrino	nephew	*la sobrina*	niece
el yerno	son-in-law	*la nuera*	daughter-in-law
el cuñado	brother-in-law	*la cuñada*	sister-in-law
el padrastro	stepdad	*la madrastra*	stepmom
el hijastro	stepson	*la hijastra*	stepdaughter

BillTalks

¡Yo hablo español!
Check the app
for more on
members of the
family.

For affection,
-ito and *-ita*
can be added
to many of these:
mi abuelita my
                grandma
mi hermanito my kid
                brother
mi bebita   my little
                baby
                girl

When both genders combine, use the "masculine" plural.
Watch:

los nietos	grandchildren
los primos	cousins
los parientes	relatives
los hijos	sons or sons and daughters
los hermanos	brothers or brothers and sisters
los papás, los padres	parents
los abuelos	grandparents
los bisabuelos	great grandparents
los padrastros	stepparents
los hijastros	stepchildren

QUICK TIPS

- The family unit is a vital part of Hispanic culture. Be sensitive.
- Other terms of endearment may be used besides the preceding words to name family members. Learn by asking or look them up if you need to.
- See how the informal *tú* is used for "you" instead of *usted* when family and friends talk to each other.
- Use *Es* a lot around *la familia*:
  Él /Ella es___.
  He's/She's___.
  mayor   older
  menor   younger
  un(a) gemelo(a)   a twin
  casado(a)   married
  soltero(a)   single
- Now, add your own "descriptive words":
  Es . . . (He/She is)   *. . . joven* (young)   *viejo(a)* old
  anciano(a) elderly

¡Mucho trabajo! (Lots of Work!)

Most folks don't spend all of their time hanging around the relatives at home. They go to work. Let's expand our "people-talk" to include the words needed to chat about our employment. Can you see a pattern here?

BillTalks
50

¡Yo hablo español! Check the app for more on occupations.

Los trabajadores (The Workers)

el/la abogado(a)	lawyer

Mi hermana es abogada en Texas.

el/la arquitecto(a)	architect
el/la bombero(a)	firefighter
el/la cajero(a)	cashier
el/la camarero(a)	waiter/waitress
el/la camionero(a)	truck driver
el/la carpintero(a)	carpenter
el/la cirujano(a)	surgeon
el/la cocinero(a)	chef
el/la doctor(a)	doctor
el/la enfermero(a)	nurse
el/la granjero(a)	farmer
el/la ingeniero(a)	engineer
el/la jardinero(a)	gardener
el/la maestro(a)	teacher
el/la mecánico(a)	mechanic
el/la músico(a)	musician
el/la obrero(a)	factory worker
el/la pintor(a)	painter
el/la plomero(a)	plumber
el/la psicólogo(a)	psychologist

el/la secretario(a)	secretary
el/la técnico(a)	technician
el/la vendedor(a)	salesperson
el/la dueño(a)	owner
el/la empleado(a)	employee
el/la empleador(a)	employer

A few don't follow the pattern above, so get ready to memorize! Pay attention!

el ayudante/la ayudanta	helper
el cliente/la clienta	client
el gerente/la gerenta	manager
el jefe/la jefa	boss
el/la agente	agent
el/la asistente	assistant
el/la dentista	dentist
el/la dependiente	clerk
el/la estudiante	student
el/la policía	police officer
el/la psiquiatra	psychiatrist
el/la soldado	soldier

CHOOSE 'N' USE!

¿Quién es . . .?	Who is (the) . . . (owner, chef, teacher, etc.)?
Tengo excelente . . .	I have an excellent . . . (assistant, doctor, lawyer, etc.).
. . . es malo/incompetente.	The . . . (painter, mechanic, actress, etc.) is terrible.

Trabajo, trabajo, trabajo

There's really no way to present all the Spanish words related to *el trabajo* because we all hold different *trabajos*. The following is a *colección* of miscellaneous stuff. If you need to know the name of something specific at your workplace, ask a Spanish speaker for some help. (Remember: *¿Qué es esto en español?* is "What is this thing called in Spanish?").

"Work" on these words!

la agencia	agency	*Necesito el número de la agencia.*
el almacén	warehouse	
el archivo	file	
el cheque	check	
la cita	appointment	
la computadora	computer	
la conferencia	conference (lecture/panel)	
el contrato	contract	
la copiadora	copier	
el correo	mail	
el entrenamiento	training	
la entrevista	interview	
la fábrica	factory	
los formularios	forms	
la habilidad	skill	
la herramienta	tool	
el horario	schedule	
la huelga	strike	
la impresora	printer	
la lista	list	
la máquina	machine	
el material	material	
la oficina	office	
la oficina principal	headquarters	
el plan	plan	
el producto	product	
el programa	program	
el proyecto	project	
la reparación	repair	
la reunión	meeting	
la seguridad	security	
el sueldo	salary	
la venta	sale	

BillTalks

51   *¡Yo hablo español!*
Check the app for
more on describing
people and things.

QUICK TIPS

- Some *descripciones* do not change because they don't end in *a* or *o*:
  Un hombre grande.
  Una señorita grande.
- Some words change a little and go immediately in front of the noun.
  Él es un buen amigo.
  He's a very good friend.
  Ella es una gran persona.   She's a great person.
  Ella está mal preparada. She is poorly prepared.
- Did you know that *los colores* are *descripción* words?
  El perro es grande y negro.   The dog is big and black.

 A different way to say the same thing above is *El hombre es grande.* And of course you'll need the *El* and *La* Business and the Once-and-for-All Rule: *Ellas son señoritas bonitas.* (They are pretty girls.)

The Good, the Bad, and the Ugly

Describing people in Spanish is no different from describing places and things. As you've discovered you can rely on the Reversal Rule! Whenever you want to add a description, simply think backwards.

Él es un	*hombre*	*grande.*
He is a	big	man.

Delve into these daily describers! Use the names of people or things:

alto(a)   tall   *Mi hermano es alto.*
bajo(a)   short (height)   *La planta es baja.*

bonito(a)	pretty	*débil*	weak
bueno(a)	good	*extraño(a)*	strange
chico(a)	small	*feo(a)*	ugly
corto(a)	short (length)	*flaco(a), delgado(a)*	thin

fuerte	strong	*nuevo(a)*	new	
gordo(a)	fat	*perezoso(a)*	lazy	
grande	big	*simpático(a)*	nice	
guapo(a)	handsome	*trabajador(a)*	hard-working	
largo(a)	long			
malo(a)	bad	*viejo(a)*	old	

"Describing" in Spanish seems strange at first, but soon, for the rest of us, our brains will make the switch automatically!

Más descripciones

Es_____.   It's/He's/She's/You're_____.

aburrido(a)	boring	*estrecho(a)*	narrow	
ancho(a)	wide	*fácil*	easy	
áspero(a)	rough	*famoso(a)*	famous	
barato(a)	inexpensive	*frío(a)*	cold	
blando(a)	soft	*inteligente*	smart	
brillante	bright	*interesante*	interesting	
caliente	hot to touch	*joven*	young	
calvo(a)	bald	*lento(a)*	slow	
caro(a)	expensive	*limpio(a)*	clean	
claro(a)	light (in color)	*lleno(a)*	full	
cobarde	cowardly	*maravilloso(a)*	wonderful	
difícil	difficult	*mayor*	older	
disponible	available	*menor*	younger	
duro(a)	hard	*moreno(a)*	dark-haired	
equivocado(a)	wrong	*oscuro(a)*	dark	

QUICK TIPS

- *Descripción* words that start with *in-* usually refer to an opposite: *correcto > incorrecto* (not correct).
- There are countless *descripciones* which are easy to recall because they're a lot like English: *favorito(a), natural, sincero(a), moderno(a), popular, elegante, terrible, furioso(a)*
- But, lookout for "fakers!" *Embarazada*, for example, doesn't mean "embarrassed" – it means "pregnant"!
- For a more complete *descripción*, do so as you would in *inglés*: The house is big, red, and green. *La casa es grande, roja y verde.*
- Many descriptions can be learned by memorizing pairs of "opposites": *grande-chico, alto-bajo,* etc.
- How detailed can you be?
  tattoo *el tatuaje*
  braids *las trenzas*
  pony tail *la cola de caballo*
  beard *la barba*
  piercing *el piercing*

Now that you are putting two or more words together on your own, here's a suggestion: be proud of yourself. Self-confidence builds from little successes. So whenever you describe anyone or anything – relax and just keep rambling on!

peligroso(a)	dangerous	*roto(a)*	broken
pelirrojo(a)	red-headed	*rubio(a)*	blonde
perdido(a)	lost	*suave*	smooth
picante	spicy hot	*sucio(a)*	dirty
pobre	poor	*tonto(a)*	dumb
rápido(a)	fast	*vacío(a)*	empty
rico(a)	rich	*valiente*	brave

Add phrases to make comparisons:

más grande que	bigger than	*Mi libro es más grande que tu libro.*
el/la más grande	biggest	*Geraldo es el más grande.*
tan grande como	as big as	*Él es tan grande como yo.*

And use "little words" to elaborate:

El estudiante es _____ *nervioso.*   *un poco*   *muy*   *demasiado*   *tan*   *más*   *menos*
The student is _____ nervous.   a little   very   too   so   more   less

CHOOSE 'n' USE!

Marco no es . . .	Marco isn't . . . (rich, bald, young, etc.).
Mi carro es tan . . .	My car is so . . . (empty, slow, dirty, etc.).
¿Qué es . . .?	What is . . . (dark, soft, etc.)?
Usted no es muy . . .	You aren't very . . . (fat, old, etc.).
Ella es . . . , . . . y . . .	She's . . . (pretty, etc.), . . . , (tall, etc.), and . . . (nice, etc.).
¿Daniel es . . . o . . .?	Is Daniel . . . (lazy, etc.) or . . . (hard-working, etc.)?

¿PUEDE RECORDARLO?
(Can You Remember It?)

☑ Explain a few of the differences between *es* and *está*

☑ Give five Spanish words that tell how you feel.

☑ Name six different body parts.

☑ Give a healthcare emergency expression in Spanish.

☑ Name five basic members of the family.

☑ Say five job titles or occupations.

☑ What are some words that refer to office work?

☑ Can you use five different descriptive words (adjectives) in short sentences?

6

CHAPTER *SEIS*

Las cosas

(Things)

"Mi casa es su casa"

As with all new words, it's best to learn these through "experience." Have a friend or another person command you to move, point to, pick up, carry, or just touch the following common household objects:

el sofá   **el sillón**   **la lámpara**

la silla   **el televisor**   **el microondas**

los cuadros   **la mesa**   **la mesita de noche**

el refrigerador   **la tina de baño**   **el librero**

Although these are okay for now, try to find other words that mean the same thing!

BillTalks

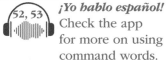
52, 53

¡Yo hablo español!
Check the app for more on using command words.

Mueva_____.	**el sofá**
Move_____.	**el sillón**
	la lámpara
Señale_____.	**la silla**
Point to_____.	**el televisor**
	el microondas
Recoja_____.	**los cuadros**
Pick up_____.	**la mesa**
	la mesita de noche
Toque_____.	**el refrigerador**
Touch_____.	**la tina de baño**
	el librero

Mire_____.
Look at_____.
Limpie_____.
Clean_____.

Touch and teach.
Add a drawing or
two, then put your
finger on each picture
as you name it!

BillTalks

54
¡Yo hablo español!
Check the app
for more on parts
of *la casa*.

la chimenea	fireplace
la cama	bed
el tocador	dressing table
la estufa	stove
el horno	oven
la alfombra	carpet
el excusado	toilet
el mostrador	counter
el lavabo	sink
el congelador	freezer
el grifo	faucet
el reloj	clock
el espejo	mirror
la ducha	shower

Stand in one place and quickly point to these!

la puerta	door
la ventana	window
el piso	floor
el techo	roof, ceiling
la pared	wall

CHOOSE 'n' USE!

. . . está sucio(a).	The . . . (lamp, refrigerator, etc.) is dirty.
No puedo encontrar . . .	I can't find the . . . (table, chair, etc.).
¿Cuánto cuesta . . .?	How much is the . . . (computer, stove, etc.)?

QUICK TIPS

- For describing more than one item, apply the "Once-and-for-All" rule: *Las puertas son blancas.*
- Review these key words before you go any further. Notice the *El* or *La* business:
  that *ese* or *esa*
  Ese piso blanco.
  these *estos* or *estas*
  Estos espejos sucios.
  this *este* or *esta*
  Esta puerta grande.
  those *esos* or *esas*
  Esas camas nuevas.
  When you don't care to be specific, use **esto** and **eso**:
  What's this? *¿Qué es esto?*
  What's that? *¿Qué es eso?*
  When the object of discussion is far away, try these:
  That book is mine.
  Aquel libro es mío.
  Those books are mine.
  Aquellos libros son míos.
  That pen is mine.
  Aquella pluma es mía.
  Those pens are mine.
  Aquellas plumas son mías.

QUICK TIPS

- Lots of household objects can be said in English and are easier if left untranslated!
  el switch   la TV   los speakers
- Discover more on your own!

¡Más cosas en la casa!

Learn all you can in sets of *cinco*:

los cestos de basura	trash cans
las cortinas	curtains
los cajones	drawers
los gabinetes	cabinets
las persianas	blinds
los cubiertos	silverware
los platillos	bowls
los platos	plates
los trastos	dishes
los vasos	drinking glasses
la cafetera	coffee maker
la lavadora	washer
la licuadora	blender
la secadora	dryer
el/la tostador(a)	toaster

¡Más aún! (More Still!)

la almohada	pillow
la cobija	blanket
el cubrecama	bedspread
la funda	pillowcase
la sábana	sheet
la aspiradora	vacuum cleaner
la escoba	broom
la plancha	iron
la tabla de planchar	ironing board
el trapeador	mop
el balde	bucket
la esponja	sponge
el jabón	soap
el limpiador	cleanser
la toalla	towel

CHOOSE 'n' USE!

No tiene un/una . . .	It doesn't have a . . . (cabinet, closet, etc.).
No me gusta el color de . . .	I don't like the color of the . . . (rugs, curtains, etc.).

¿Dónde está? (Where Is It?)

Next time you can't find what you're looking for around *la casa*, send out a search party *en español*! Here are a few places where it's most likely to be found.

BillTalks

55

¡Yo hablo español! Check the app for more on making location sentences with *está*.

*Está en*____.	It's (in, on, or at) the____.
el apartamento	apartment
el césped	grass, lawn
la cocina	kitchen
el comedor	dining room
el cuarto	room
el cuarto de baño	bathroom
el desván	attic
el dormitorio	bedroom
las escaleras	stairs
el garaje	garage
el jardín	garden
el pasillo	hallway
el ropero	closet
la sala	living room
el sótano	basement

Vocabulario especial (Special Vocabulary)

These *frases* will get you speaking *muy rápido:*

*Voy a buscar*____.	I'm going to look for (the)____.
*No tengo*____.	I don't have (the)____.
*Necesito*____.	I need (the)____.

el aire acondicionado	air conditioning	*No tengo el aire acondicionado.*
la calefacción	heating	
la cerca	fence	
la electricidad	electricity	

el portón	gate
el sistema de seguridad	security system
el timbre	doorbell
la tubería	plumbing
las cerraduras	locks

Voy a buscar las llaves.

los enchufes	outlets
las llaves	keys
las luces	lights
los muebles	furniture
las repisas	shelves

BillTalks

56

¡Yo hablo español! Check the app for more on household vocabulary.

CHOOSE 'n' USE!

Voy a revisar . . .	I'm going to check (the) . . . (furniture, locks etc.).
Hay un/una . . .	There's a . . . (basement, attic, etc.).
¿Puede reparar . . .?	Can you repair . . . (the plumbing, stairs, etc.)?

QUICK TIP

Try these wonderful one-liners.
Se me perdió.	I lost it.
Se me olvidó.	I forgot it.
Se me rompió.	I broke it.

Las herramientas (Tools)

Tráigame . . .	Bring me (the) . . .	
el alicate	pliers	*Tráigame el alicate grande.*
la brocha	paint brush	
la cinta	tape	
el clavo	nail	
el destornillador	screwdriver	
la escalera	ladder	
la llave inglesa	wrench	
la manguera	hose	
el martillo	hammer	
la pala	shovel	
la pintura	paint	

el rastrillo	rake
el serrucho	saw
las tijeras	scissors
el tornillo	screw

Los materiales (Materials)

el acero	steel	***Tráigame la puerta de acero.***
el alambre	wire	
el asfalto	asphalt	
la baldosa	floor tile	
el cartón	cardboard	
el cemento	cement	
el cobre	copper	
la goma	rubber	
el hierro	iron	
el ladrillo	brick	
la madera	wood	
el metal	metal	
el plástico	plastic	
la piedra	stone	
la tela	cloth	

La vida en la ciudad (Life in the City)

BillTalks

57

¡Yo hablo español! Check the app for more on city buildings.

Spanish fills our cities, so let's leave the comfy confines of *la casa* and head into town. Walk, ride, or drive around pointing and naming things. (If you're caught talking to yourself, don't stop! It'll be too hard to explain.)

Los edificios (Buildings)

el almacén	warehouse	*Ella no está en el almacén.*
el banco	bank	
la biblioteca	library	
el cine	movie theater	
el correo	post office	
el departamento de bomberos	fire department	
la escuela	school	
la estación de policía	police station	
el café	coffee shop	
la fábrica	factory	
la farmacia	pharmacy	
la gasolinera	gas station	
el hospital	hospital	
la iglesia	church	
el museo	museum	
la oficina	office	
el restaurante	restaurant	
el supermercado	supermarket	
la tienda	store	

Los lugares y sitios (Places and Sites)

la acera	sidewalk	*Estoy en la acera.*
el aeropuerto	airport	
el ascensor	elevator	
la calle	street	
el camino	road	
la carretera	highway	
el centro	downtown	
el centro comercial	mall	
la cuadra	city block	
la esquina	corner	
el estacionamiento	parking lot	
el parque	park	
el puente	bridge	
el vecindario	neighborhood	

The way to say "town" is **"el pueblo."**

Keep looking around:

el semáforo	traffic light
el buzón	mailbox
la parada de autobús	bus stop

CHOOSE 'n' USE!

¿Sabe dónde está . . .?	Do you know where the . . . (museum, bank, etc.) is?
. . . está cerca de . . .	The . . . (church, etc.) is near the . . . (school, etc.).
Espéreme Ud. en . . .	Wait for me at the . . . (subway, corner, etc.).

El transporte (Transportation)

el autobús	bus	*Necesito el autobús número 25.*
el avión	airplane	
el barco	boat	
la bicicleta	bicycle	
el camión	truck	
el carro or *el coche*	car	
el helicóptero	helicopter	
el metro	metro	
el tren	train	

BillTalks

58

¡Yo hablo español! Check the app for more on city survival words.

Just use English to say "Taxi!" or request an "Uber."

CHOOSE 'n' USE!

¿Va en . . . o . . .?	Are you going by . . . (car, etc.) or . . . (train, etc.)?
No me gusta viajar en . . .	I don't like traveling by . . . (airplane, etc.).
Busco . . .	I'm looking for the . . . (bus, etc.).

Más City Life

las afueras	outskirts	*Mi casa está en las afueras de la ciudad.*
el campamento	campgrounds	
la cantina	bar	
la cárcel	jail	
el cementerio	cemetery	
el lote de carros	car lot	
la piscina	pool	
el rascacielos	skyscraper	
el zoológico	zoo	

There is a little piece of language *-ería* (pronounced air-EE-ah) that is found at the end of words which name stores and shops. Watch the pattern:

la carnicería	meat market	***Vamos a la carnicería.***
la joyería	jewelry store	
la juguetería	toy store	
la mueblería	furniture store	
la panadería	bakery	
la peluquería	hair salon	
la zapatería	shoe store	

As you travelers can see, the *-ería* ending will work wonders for you as you're finding your way around *la ciudad*.

You may also need these:

Las direcciones

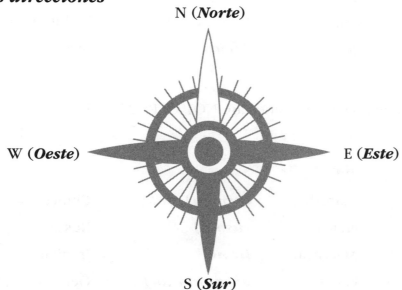

N (*Norte*)

W (*Oeste*)

E (*Este*)

S (*Sur*)

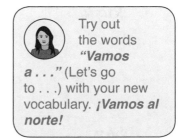

Try out the words *"Vamos a . . ."* (Let's go to . . .) with your new vocabulary. *¡Vamos al norte!*

Now, fill out that form, telling where you live:

el condado	county	_____
el estado	state	_____
el país	country	_____

Unas naciones y nacionalidades
(Some Countries and Nationalities)

Meeting people from many different parts of the world is becoming increasingly common. Here are some words to give your Spanish conversation an international flair.

¿Es usted de___?	Are you from___?		
España	Spain	Irán	Iran
Francia	France	Alemania	Germany
los Estados Unidos	the United States (EE.UU. = USA)	Italia	Italy
		Canadá	Canada
		Centroamérica	Central America
Inglaterra	England	Norteamérica	North America
Irlanda	Ireland	Sudamérica	South America
Japón	Japan	Europa	Europe
China	China	Oriente Medio	Middle East
Rusia	Russia	África	Africa

See how nationalities are NOT CAPITALIZED.

Soy___.	I'm___.		
español(ola)	Spanish	chino(a)	Chinese
francés(-esa)	French	ruso(a)	Russian
americano(a)	American	iraní	Iranian
inglés(-esa)	English	alemán(-ana)	German
irlandés(-esa)	Irish	italiano(a)	Italian
japonés(-esa)	Japanese	canadiense	Canadian

Spanish-Speaking Countries and Nationalities in Latin America

Can you find these on a map? Careful – they're all in Spanish!

la Argentina	*argentino(a)*	*México*	*mejicano(a)*
Bolivia	*boliviano(a)*	*Nicaragua*	*nicaragüense*
Chile	*chileno(a)*	*Panamá*	*panameño(a)*
Colombia	*colombiano(a)*	*el Paraguay*	*paraguayo(a)*
Costa Rica	*costarricense*	*el Perú*	*peruano(a)*
Cuba	*cubano(a)*	*Puerto Rico*	*puertorriqueño(a)*
el Ecuador	*ecuatoriano(a)*	*la República Dominicana*	*dominicano(a)*
El Salvador	*salvadoreño(a)*	*el Uruguay*	*uruguayo(a)*
Guatemala	*guatemalteco(a)*	*Venezuela*	*venezolano(a)*
Honduras	*hondureño(a)*		

QUICK TIPS

- Unlike in English, nationalities are not capitalized!
  La frontera is "the border."
- Continue to practice your *pregunta* words:
  ¿Adónde va Ud.?
  Where are you going?
  ¡Voy a hacer un viaje!
  I'm taking a trip!

¡Los grupos raciales/étnicos!
(Racial/Ethnic Groups)

asiático(a)	Asian *Soy asiático.*
blanco(a)	White
afroamericano(a)	African American
indio(a) or *amerindio(a)*	Native American
hispano(a) or *latino(a)*	Hispanic or Latin American

CHOOSE 'n' USE!

Me voy a mudar a . . .	I'm moving to . . .
Está en la frontera de . . .	It's on the border of . . .
¿Ha ido a . . .?	Have you been to . . .?

La naturaleza
(Nature)

Let's get out of town for a while! But before we take off, why don't we "handle" a few of nature's little wonders that are within "reach" – right outside the door! And as we do with all new words of objects – let's "touch 'n talk".

*Mire*____.	Look at (the)____.
el árbol	tree
el arbusto	bush
la arena	sand
la flor	flower
el pasto	grass
la hoja	leaf
el lodo	mud
el palo	stick
la piedra	rock
la planta	plant
el polvo	dust
la rama	branch
la semilla	seed
la tierra	dirt

BillTalks
59 *¡Yo hablo español!* Check the app for more on the countryside.

Los insectos	(Insects)
la abeja	bee
la araña	spider
la avispa	wasp
el caracol	snail
la cucaracha	cockroach
el grillo	cricket
la hormiga	ant
la mosca	fly
el zancudo	mosquito

BillTalks
60 *¡Yo hablo español!* Check the app for more countryside vocabulary.

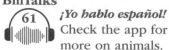

BillTalks
61
¡Yo hablo español!
Check the app for
more on animals.

Muchos animales (A lot of Animals)

Los domésticos **(The "Domestic Ones")**

el caballo	horse	*Mi amigo tiene dos caballos negros.*
el chivo	goat	
el conejo	rabbit	
el gallo	rooster	
el gato	cat	
la oveja	sheep	
el pájaro	bird	
el pato	duck	
el perro	dog	
el pez	fish	
el pollo	chicken	
el puerco	pig	
el ratón	mouse	
la tortuga	turtle	
la vaca	cow	

Los salvajes **(The "Wild Ones")**

el águila	eagle	*El águila es mi animal favorito.*
el camello	camel	
la cebra	zebra	
el elefante	elephant	
el gorila	gorilla	
el hipopótamo	hippopotamus	
la jirafa	giraffe	
el león	lion	
el lobo	wolf	
el mono	monkey	
el oso	bear	
el rinoceronte	rhinoceros	
el tigre	tiger	
el venado	deer	
la víbora	snake	

CHOOSE 'n' USE!

Hay . . . allí.	There's . . . (a flower, a goat, etc.) over there.
¿Tiene . . .?	Does it have . . .? (bushes, chickens, etc.)?
No me gusta . . .	I don't like . . . (mud, spiders, etc.).
¿Ha visto . . .?	Have you seen the . . . (rock, camel, etc.)?
. . . es mi favorito(a).	The . . . (tiger, tree, etc.) is my favorite.
. . . no es peligroso(a).	The . . . (zebra, etc.) isn't dangerous.
. . . come mucho.	The . . . (bear, lion, etc.) eats a lot.
. . . es inteligente.	The . . . (monkey, dog, etc.) is smart.
. . . vive en la selva.	The . . . (hippopotamus, etc.) lives in the jungle.

Más lugares (More Places)

Now let our words head for *el campo* (the countryside).

BillTalks

62 *¡Yo hablo español!* Check the app for describing more of the countryside.

Vamos a___.	Let's go to (the)___.
el bosque	forest
el cerro	hill
la costa	coast
el desierto	desert
el lago	lake
el mar	sea
la montaña	mountain
la playa	beach
el arroyo	stream
el río	river
la selva	jungle
el valle	valley
la cueva	cave
la finca	farm
el rancho	ranch
la cabaña	cabin

CHOOSE 'n' USE!

. . . es maravilloso(a).	The (ranch, coast, etc.) is marvelous.
Ellos viven en . . .	They live in the . . . (valley, ocean, etc.).
¡Vamos a . . .!	Let's go to the . . . (lake, desert, etc.)!

¡Tengo hambre!
(I'm Hungry!)

Food words, too, may differ slightly from region to region, but don't get nervous; instead, eat and ask! The words that follow can be used safely everywhere!

¡La comida! (Food!)

el arroz	rice	*el jamón*	ham
Quiero el arroz blanco.		*la langosta*	lobster
		la mantequilla	butter
el bistec	steak	*la nuez*	nut
el camarón	shrimp	*el pan*	bread
el cangrejo	crab	*el pastel*	pie
la carne	meat	*el pavo*	turkey
el cerdo	pork	*el perro caliente*	hot dog
el cereal	cereal	*el pescado*	fish
el chicle	gum	*el pollo*	chicken
el dulce	candy	*el queso*	cheese
la ensalada	salad	*la salchicha*	sausage
el fideo	noodle	*la sopa*	soup
la galleta	cookie	*la soya*	soy
la hamburguesa	hamburger	*el tocino*	bacon
el helado	ice cream	*la torta*	cake
el huevo	egg		

Las frutas (Fruit)

la cereza	cherry	*el melocotón*	peach
No me gusta la cereza.		*la naranja*	orange
		la pera	pear
el coco	coconut	*la piña*	pineapple
la fresa	strawberry	*el plátano*	banana
el limón	lemon	*la toronja*	grapefruit
la manzana	apple	*la uva*	grape

Los vegetales (Vegetables)

el apio	celery	*la lechuga*	lettuce
Necesito la sopa de apio.		*el maíz*	corn
		la patata or *papa*	potato
la calabaza	squash	*el pepino*	cucumber
la cebolla	onion	*el tomate*	tomato
la col or *el repollo*	cabbage	*la zanahoria*	carrot
la espinaca	spinach	*los guisantes*	
los frijoles	beans	or *chícharos*	pea

La nutrición

Healthy living helps, so why not work on that *dieta en español!*

Necesito más___.	I need more___.
comida sana	healthy food
comidas orgánicas	organic food
fibra	fiber
granos integrales	whole grains
minerales	minerals
proteínas	protein
vitaminas	vitamins

Try to mumble these words before you dig in!

Necesito menos___.	I need less___.
calorías	calories
carbohidratos	carbohydrates
comida basura	junk food
comidas procesadas	processed food
grasa	fat

La cocina (The Kitchen)

el abrelatas	can opener
el delantal	apron
el mantel	tablecloth
el sartén	frying pan
la olla	pot
la receta	recipe

CHOOSE 'n' USE!

La ensalada tiene . . .	The salad has . . . (carrots, onions, etc.).
¡ . . . es dulce!	The . . . (corn, orange, etc.) is sweet!
No puedo comer . . .	I can't eat . . . (lemons, strawberries, etc.).
¿Quisiera una . . . o . . .?	Would you like a . . . (banana, etc.) or a . . . (grapefruit, etc.)?
. . . huele mal.	The . . . (lettuce, etc.) smells bad.
¿Necesita . . .?	Do you need a . . . (tablecloth, etc.)?
¡Qué ___!	How ___!
delicioso/a	delicious
sabroso/a	tasty
¡Está muy ___!	It's very ___!
picante	hot (to taste)
caliente	hot (to touch)
Voy a comprar ___	I'm going to buy ___ (taco, etc.).

Restaurante Remarks

Quisiera____.	I'd like____.
Ella tiene____.	She has____.
Tráigame____	Bring me____
algo de comer.	something to eat.
algo de beber.	something to drink.
el plato del día.	today's special.
el menú.	a menu.
más agua.	more water.
la cuenta.	the bill.
el postre.	the dessert.
el aperitivo.	the appetizer.

Tráigame algo de comer, por favor.

Menú

¿Está ___?	**Is it ___?**
asado(a)	roasted
cocido(a)	cooked
crudo(a)	raw
fresco(a)	fresh
frito(a)	fried
hervido(a)	boiled
maduro(a)	ripe
podrido(a)	rotten

¿Está asado el pollo?

Now munch on these helpful tidbits:

Estoy a dieta.	I'm on a diet.
Para comer aquí.	To eat here.
Para llevar.	To go.
Quiero ordenar.	I want to order.
La cuenta, por favor.	Check, please.

BillTalks
63 *¡Yo hablo español!* Check the app for more on food.

Las comidas	**(The Meals)**
el desayuno	breakfast
el almuerzo	lunch
la cena	dinner

Eat up these important words:

la camarera or *mesera*	waitress
el camarero or *mesero*	waiter
el/la cocinero(a)	cook

Necesito . . .	I need the . . .
la cuchara	spoon

Necesito la cuchara grande, por favor.

el cuchillo	knife
el platillo	saucer
el plato	plate
el pimentero	pepper shaker
la servilleta	napkin
la taza	cup
el tenedor	fork
el salero	salt shaker
el vaso	glass
la botella	bottle

Tengo sed (I'm Thirsty)

Quiero___.	I want the___.
el batido	milkshake/smoothie

Quiero el batido de fresa.

la bebida	drink
el café	coffee
el café descafeinado	decaffeinated coffee
la cerveza	beer
el hielo	ice
el jugo	juice
la leche	milk
la limonada	lemonade
el refresco	soft drink
el té	tea
el vino	wine

BillTalks

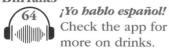

¡Yo hablo español! Check the app for more on drinks.

Los sabores (Flavors)

Está___.	It's___.
dulce	sweet
amargo(a)	bitter
agrio(a)	sour
seco(a)	dry
salado(a)	salty

BillTalks
65
¡Yo hablo español!
Check the app for
more on *hay*
(there is/are).

Los ingredientes (Ingredients)

Tengo____.	I have the____.
el aceite	oil
el ajo	garlic
el azúcar	sugar
la canela	cinnamon
el condimento	spice
la crema	cream
la harina	flour
el jarabe	syrup
la miel	honey
la mostaza	mustard
la pimienta	pepper
la sal	salt
la salsa	sauce
la vainilla	vanilla
el vinagre	vinegar

QUICK TIPS

- Use *mucho* and *poco* for a large and small "amount." *Muchos* and *pocos* are for many and a few!
- *el* or *la bartender* is easy to remember

CHOOSE 'n' USE!

Necesito . . .	I need the . . . (waiter, napkin, etc.).
. . . está sucio(a).	The . . . (glass, fork, etc.) is dirty.
Se me cayó . . .	I dropped the . . . (spoon, cup, etc.).
Necesita más . . .	It needs more . . . (sauce, mustard, etc.).
Hay demasiado(a) . . .	There's too much . . . (salt, garlic, etc.).
No bebo . . .	I don't drink . . . (wine, juice, etc.).
¿Quiere Ud. . . . o . . .?	Do you want . . . (coffee) or . . . (tea)?
. . . está horrible.	The . . . (drink, etc.) is horrible.

¿Qué lleva puesto? (What Are You Wearing?)

BillTalks

66

¡Yo hablo español!
Check the app for
more on clothing.

Get dressed in Spanish! The next time you're putting something on, name it *en español*!

La ropa	(Clothing)
el abrigo	overcoat
la bata de baño	bathrobe
la blusa	blouse
las botas	boots
las bragas	panties
la bufanda	scarf
los calcetines	socks
los calzoncillos	shorts
la camisa	shirt
la camiseta	T-shirt
la chaqueta	jacket
el cinturón	belt
la corbata	tie
la falda	skirt
la gorra	cap
los guantes	gloves
el impermeable	raincoat
las medias	stockings
los pantalones	pants
el pijama	pajamas
la ropa interior	underwear
el saco	sportscoat
el sombrero	hat
la sudadera	sweatshirt
el suéter	sweater
los tenis	tennis shoes
el traje	suit
el traje de baño	bathing suit
el vestido	dress
las zapatillas	slippers
los zapatos	shoes

¿Dónde está el abrigo negro?

QUICK TIPS

- Use these *palabras* at the department store:
  La ropa
  . . . para mujeres
  women's clothing
  . . . para hombres
  men's clothing
  . . . para niños
  children's clothing
- You may need a few "clothing commands," too:
  ¡Quítese la ropa!
  Take off your clothes!
  ¡Vístase! Get dressed!
  ¡Póngaselo! Put it on!
- *Más cosas importantes:*
  el botón button
  el bolsillo pocket
  el cierre zipper
- *Un par de* is "a pair of" *Un par de zapatos*

Describe clothes with *los colores: Son pantalones azules*.

CHOOSE 'n' USE!

¿Dónde compró Ud . . .?	Where did you buy the . . . (jacket, shirt, etc.)?
Me gusta el color de . . .	I like the color of the . . . (blouse, pants, etc.).
Necesito . . .	I need the . . . (slippers, suit, etc.).
¿Cuánto cuesta . . .?	How much is the . . . (dress, overcoat, etc.)?
. . . son muy viejos(as).	The . . . (shoes, shorts, etc.) are very old.

Lavar la ropa (Washing Clothes)

"The cleaners" are *la lavandería*.
"Dirty laundry" is *la ropa sucia*.
"Detergent" is *el detergente*.
"Stain" is *la mancha*.
"Bleach" is *el blanqueador*.
"Hangers" are *los ganchos*.

 You may hear different words used to name these things. Who cares? These will work fine for now!

BillTalks

67 *¡Yo hablo español!* Check the app to review what you have studied so far.

¿PUEDE RECORDARLO?
(Can You Remember It?)

In Spanish:
- ☑ Name three job titles.
- ☑ Name three descriptive words.
- ☑ Name three pieces of furniture.
- ☑ Name three rooms in the house.
- ☑ Name three buildings in the city.
- ☑ Name three plants or animals.
- ☑ Name three foods or beverages.
- ☑ Name three articles of clothing.

¡*Vamos de compras!* (Let's Go Shopping!)

Whether in store or online, you'll probably need your **la tarjeta de crédito** (credit card), along with these other important **palabras**:

el cambio	change	***Aquí tiene su cambio.***
el cheque	check	
la cuenta	bill	
el cupón	coupon	
el débito	debit	
el descuento	discount	
el dinero	money	
la ganga	bargain	
el trato	deal	
la oferta	offer	
el pago	payment	
el precio	price	
el recibo	receipt	
la venta	sale	

La joyería (Jewelry Store)

el anillo	ring	***¡Me gusta mucho el anillo grande!***
los aretes	earrings	
el brazalete	bracelet	
el broche	brooch	
la cadena	chain	
el collar	necklace	
los diamantes	diamonds	

las joyas	jewels
el oro	gold
las perlas	pearls
la plata	silver
el reloj	watch

Buyers Babble!

¿Es todo?	Is that all?
¡Me encanta!	I love it!
¿Qué marca es?	What brand is it?
No me queda bien.	It doesn't fit.
Me quedo con esto.	I'll take this.
¿Cuánto cuesta? (or *vale*?)	How much is it?
¿Cuánto pesa?	How much does it weigh?
Quiero probármelo(a).	I want to try it on.
Quiero cargarlo(a) a mi cuenta.	I want to charge it to my account.
¿En qué puedo servirle?	How can I help you?
¿Algo más?	Something else?
¿Cuánto por ciento?	What percent?
Soy miembro.	I'm a member.
Es gratis.	It's free.
Necesito un(a) dependiente.	I need a clerk.
Quiero un(a) cajero(a).	I want a cashier.
¿Cuál departamento?	Which department?

¿Cuál es su talla? (What's Your Size?)

Uso un___.	I take a___.
chico(a)	small
mediano(a)	medium
grande	large
extragrande	X large
chiquito(a)	petite

Unas extras

la bolsa	bag, purse
la canasta	basket
la caja	box
la cartera	wallet
el cepillo	brush
la cinta	ribbon
el espejo	mirror
la maleta	suitcase
el maletín	briefcase
el maquillaje	makeup
la mochila	backpack
el paraguas	umbrella
el peine	comb
el perfume	perfume

CHOOSE 'n' USE!

Busco . . .	I am looking for the . . . (sale, perfume, etc.).
Quisiera . . .	I'd like the . . . (receipt, change, etc.).
¿Se vende . . .?	Do you sell . . . (rings, combs, etc.)?
¿Dónde están . . .?	Where are the . . . (suitcases, diamonds, etc.)?
No hay . . .	There's no . . . (mirror, basket, etc.).

"Get into the Act!"

There's no better way to learn than by doing. That is why the best language programs include commands as a method to teach both actions as well as objects.

¡Prenda la música! Turn on the music!
¡Cante la canción! Sing the song!
¡Salude a la bandera! Salute the flag!

Commands involve both the speaker and the listener.

la pantalla

With friends and family, take turns giving each other ***mandatos*** (commands). Select common objects, and using the commands below, act them out! They're great for work or play! Watch:

Apague Turn off		***Mueva*** Move	
Baje Lower		***Prenda*** Turn on	
Levante Raise		***Señale*** Point to	
Lleve Carry		***Toque*** Touch	
Mire Watch		***Traiga*** Bring	
Mire la pantalla.			

BillTalks

68 Check the app for using commands around town.

¡Más mandatos!

Baile	Dance	***Lea***	Read
Busque	Look for	***Limpie***	Clean
Cante	Sing	***Llame***	Call
Coma	Eat	***Mande***	Send
Compre	Buy	***Marque***	Dial
Escriba	Write	***Meta***	Put inside
Escuche	Listen	***Pida***	Ask for
Estudie	Study	***Quite***	Take away
Firme	Sign	***Regrese***	Return
Lave	Wash	***Repita***	Repeat

Saque	Take out	*Tome*	Drink
Siga	Continue	*Vea*	See
Suba	Climb	*Venda*	Sell
Tire	Throw	*Venga*	Come

Let's make a *mandato*!

A simple approach to forming a command in Spanish requires knowledge of the three different action word (verb) endings. The endings are:

-ar as in **hablar**	to speak
-er as in **comer**	to eat
-ir as in **escribir**	to write

To make a **mandato**, drop the last two letters of the infinitive ("to") form and replace them as follows:

$$a \rightarrow e$$

hablar → *¡Hable!* Speak!

$$er \rightarrow a$$

comer → *¡Coma!* Eat!

$$i \rightarrow a$$

escribir → *¡Escriba!* Write!

But beware! Some verbs are weird and simply have to be memorized.

ir → *¡Vaya!* Go!

venir → *¡Venga!* Come!

decir → *¡Diga!* Tell!

QUICK TIPS

- Because commands are exchanged so often between friends, you may hear folks using the *tú* (or informal) form of the action words. Don't get excited. Here are a few common "informal" commands:
  ¡Ven! Come here!
  ¡Vete! Go away!
  ¡Dime! Tell me!
  ¡Espera! Wait!
  ¡Cállate! Shut up!
  ¡Llámame! Call me!
- Use the previously listed commands for now, and don't worry about forming your own yet. You'll get the idea with practice!
- To tell someone not to do something, just put no in front of the command!
  ¡No hable!
- When you can't remember the name of an object, use *esto* for "this thing" or *eso* for "that thing."
  Lleve esto y traiga eso.
  Carry this and bring that.
- You can always get your idea across by simply using the basic action (verb) form preceded by **Hágame el favor de** (please):
  Hágame el favor de hablar.
  Please speak.
  Hágame el favor de continuar.
  Please continue.
- Start now by following these simple commands!
  ¡Toque el libro!
  Touch the book!
  ¡Escriba su nombre!
  Write your name!
  ¡Baile salsa!
  Dance the salsa!

BillTalks

69 *¡Yo hablo español!* Check the app for more on actions in Spanish.

¡Los Mighty *mandatos*!

Here are some common commands that are almost always given alone, and they work well all by themselves! (They are actually two words rolled into one.)

¡Acuéstese!	Lie down!
¡Agárrelo(a,os,as)!	Grab it/them!
¡Cálmese!	Calm down!
¡Créame!	Believe me!
¡Cuídese!	Take care of yourself!
¡Déjelo(a,os,as)!	Leave it/them alone!
¡Démelo(a,os,as)!	Give it/them to me!
¡Despiértese!	Wake up!
Lávese las manos.	Wash your hands.
No se toque la cara.	Don't touch your face.
Póngase la máscara.	Put on the mask.

As you speak, help convey meaning through facial expressions and body language.

QUICK TIPS

- Remember – inside each command is an action word! (Using commands will help you learn the Spanish verbs.)
- As you "command" and "order folks around," be nice! Add *por favor* (please) and *gracias* (thanks). And smile!
- Watch out for those accent marks! That part of the word must be said louder!
- Don't try to figure out *se, lo, me,* and the other "little endings." You'll get their meanings as you speak more. So for now, practice each command as you did the one-liners.
- Pick one command to play with each day! They're best for commanding one person only! To tell a group to do something, add an *n* to the action word: *¡Señalen!* means "You guys, point!"

BillTalks

70 *¡Yo hablo español!* Check the app for more on using command words with food and drink.

¿PUEDE RECORDARLO?
(Can You Remember It?)

In Spanish . . .

- ☑ Identify five common household items.
- ☑ Name three rooms found in most homes.
- ☑ List three different tools or building materials.
- ☑ Say the names of five common buildings you see in a major city.
- ☑ How do you say "The United States" in Spanish?
- ☑ What are three things you may find in a garden?
- ☑ List as many animals as you can.
- ☑ List as many foods and drinks as you can.
- ☑ List as many clothing items as you can.
- ☑ What are some things you might need to say when you go shopping?
- ☑ How do you make a command word out of the word *comer* (to eat)?

7

CHAPTER *SIETE*

¡ACCIÓN!

(ACTION!)

Un anuncio importante

 Spanish is easy! Most action words have the same base form. This means that all you have to do to understand action words is focus on the first (base) part of the word. Here's how it works: First, take a typical action, like "to work" *trabajar*. Now let's see what the base *trabaj-* can do!

¡Trabaj-e! (Work!)

¡Trabaj-é! (I worked!)

¡Trabaj-o! (I work!)

¡Trabaj-ando! (Working!)

¡Trabaj-aba! (I used to work!)

¡Trabaj-aría! (I would work!)

> You are about to enter the next level of proficiency in Spanish, so please read carefully . . .

This chapter introduces Spanish action words or verbs. Do not be afraid! There is no "conjugating." Instead, general suggestions are made, and practical action word lists are presented here. But you still have to pay attention. Believe it or not, this stuff is what makes Spanish really work!

As always, mistakes are good, so don't hold back. Keep a positive attitude, and do the best you can. Don't worry about every word! Use only what you need.

Basics in Action

There are only three action word endings. The basic word-forms (infinitives) end in *-ar*, *-er* or *-ir*. That's it. Learn some of the popular ones and you'll be fine. You won't always be correct, but people will still understand. To get "extensive training" in action words (verbs), buy a textbook, or take a class. But for simple communication, try to pick up on the vocabulary and tips that follow.

BillTalks

 71, 72 *¡Yo hablo español!* Check the app for more on using **-ar** verbs.

Check the app for more on using **-er** and **-ir** verbs.

A Big Step Toward Fluency

Words and one-liners are great, if you like to keep things short. But to make a Spanish conversation last, sooner or later you'll need the "to be" verbs, *estar* and *ser* ("The Big 8"). You read a little about them back in Chapter *CINCO*.

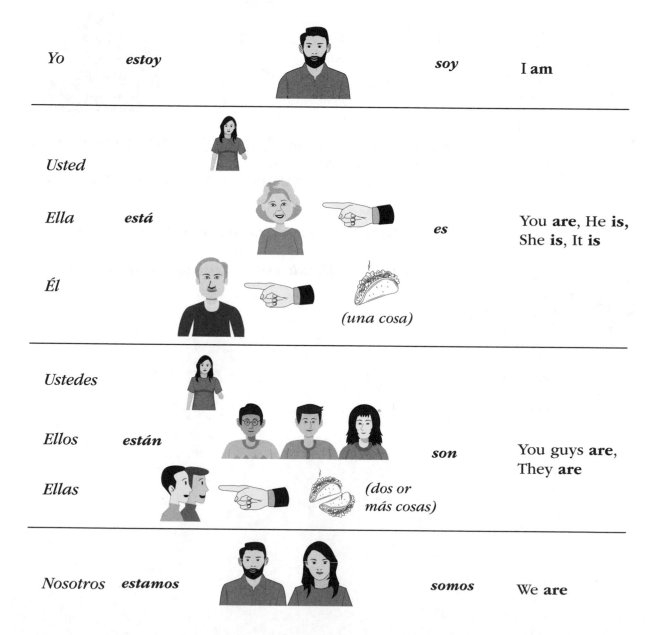

Yo	*estoy*		*soy*	I **am**
Usted				
Ella	*está*		*es*	You **are**, He **is**, She **is**, It **is**
Él		*(una cosa)*		
Ustedes				
Ellos	*están*		*son*	You guys **are**, They **are**
Ellas		*(dos or más cosas)*		
Nosotros	*estamos*		*somos*	We **are**

QUICK TIPS

- See how all these forms begin the same?

  EST . . .   oy
  EST . . .   á
  EST . . .   án
  EST . . .   amos

- *Estás* is used with *tú*. (It means "You are" among friends or family members.)

- *Esta* without the accent mark (´) means "This". *Esta es una mesa.* This is a table.

- "Think" a bit before you use them. Put your words together just as you do in *inglés*:
  I am happy.   *Yo estoy contento.* (condition)
  The chair is over there. *La silla está allí.* (location)

Check back on *Es* vs. *está* until it really sinks in! Now, take *un momento* to read the next few pages with care!

Estar

estoy	I **am**
está	you **are**, he **is**, she **is**, it **is**
están	you guys **are**, they **are**
estamos	we **are**

Knowing these four magic words will make the difference!

Chances are you're already using these TO BE words! If not, here it is in capsule form:

ESTAR can mean AM, IS, or ARE when talking about either . . .

CONDITION: *¿Cómo está usted? Estoy bien, gracias.*

or

LOCATION: *¿Dónde está usted? Estoy en la casa.*

Ser

The other "to be" word is **ser** and it's BIG-TIME! See how weird it is! You'll just have to watch closely. Trust me. It's worth it!

soy	I **am**
es	you **are**, he **is**, she **is**, it **is**
son	you guys **are**, they **are**
somos	we **are**

Instead of LOCATION or CONDITION, **Ser** words relate to:

the time	occupation
names	nationality
origin	description

Read these examples. You should be able to translate:

Soy Tony.

Es italiano.

Somos dentistas.

El carro es de metal.

Son buenos amigos.

Son las ocho de la noche.

Es muy grande.

Soy de Ecuador.

Es de día.

Es guacamole.

La Pepsi es para mí.

"To Be or Not To Be"

BillTalks

73
¡Yo hablo español! Check the app for more on expanding your conversation with *estar* and *ser*.

ESTAR
For location and condition (at this moment).

SER
For qualities, characteristics, and everything else!

Look closely, *amigos*! You've only got **EIGHT WORDS** to remember, and they don't ever change. Use this as a "study chart":

QUICK TIPS

- To ask questions, simply add question marks before and after:
  María es bonita.
  Mary is pretty.
  ¿María es bonita?
  Is Mary pretty?
- Or, if you'd like, the subject in question can be moved to the end: *¿Es bonita María?* (Word order in Spanish won't really hurt the message.)
- The informal "you" form of *ser* is *eres*.
  ¡Tú eres mi amigo!
  You are my friend!

estoy		*soy*
está		*es*
están		*son*
estamos		*somos*

Notice *la diferencia*!

Remember you can always drop the "*Quién*" words if you like!

Estar

Yo estoy aquí.	I'm here.
Ella está bien.	She's fine.
Los niños están ocupados.	The kids are busy.
Nosotros estamos trabajando.	We're working.

Ser

Yo soy Tony.	I'm Tony.
Ella es de la Argentina.	She's from Argentina.
Mis hermanos son altos.	My siblings are tall.
Nosotros somos dentistas.	We're dentists.

BillTalks

 74 *¡Yo hablo español!* Check the app for a short story: how much do you understand?

DO IT NOW!

By fooling around with these ASAP, the rest of us (who always get confused) can immediately begin sending complete messages. Do it now! You'll be amazed at how much better your Spanish will be!

BillTalks

 75 *¡Yo hablo español!* Check the app to review what you've learned.

español	*inglés*
Gabriel está en la cocina.	Gabriel is in the kitchen.
Ellos son inteligentes.	_____
Yo estoy bien.	_____
Somos bolivianos.	_____
Estamos muy contentos.	_____
Soy el presidente.	_____

Just Say "No"!

What is truly *magnífico* about *el español* is that there are so many shortcuts to success! As we've seen, to say "not" in Spanish, it's no big deal. Do nothing more than place a *no* in front of whatever it is you're trying to say.

El animal es muy grande.	*El animal <u>no</u> es muy grande.*

And no matter how complex the action, to say "not" just say, *no*!

> *¡Ella no quiere leer libros y escribir ejercicios!*
> She does not want to read books and write exercises!

Take a second to scan these *muy* useful *no-no*'s:

QUICK TIP

In Spanish, when answering questions, you need a double "no": *¿Está Juan? No, no está.* (Is John here? No, he is not.) For words like *nadie* (nobody), put *no* in front of the verb: *No está nadie.* (Nobody is here.)

No . . .		
	hay.	There isn't or aren't any.
	importa.	It's not important.
	me interesa.	I'm not interested.
	le haga caso.	Don't pay any attention.
	me di cuenta.	I didn't realize.
	lo aguanto.	I can't stand it.
	se preocupe.	Don't worry.
	sé.	I don't know.
	puede ser.	It can't be.
	me gusta.	I don't like it.

Now, what can you learn about "everyday actions" from these next examples? That's right. The "*o*" ending refers to "I."

No puedo.	I can't.	
No recuerdo.	I don't remember.	
No entiendo.	I don't understand.	
No veo.	I don't see . . .	*No veo la foto.*
No encuentro . . .	I can't find . . .	
No tengo . . .	I don't have . . .	
No quiero . . .	I don't want . . .	
No necesito . . .	I don't need . . .	

Let's *Tengo!*

BillTalks
76 *¡Yo hablo español!*
Check the app for
more on patterns
with *tiene*.

Here's another "power play" *en español*, and truly a must
for the rookie. Whenever you'd like to talk about "who has
what," use the action word *tener* (to have).

	TENER to have		
Yo	*tengo*	I **have**	*Yo tengo el libro de español.*
Usted *Él* *Ella*	*tiene*	You **have**, He, She, It **has**	*Ella tiene problemas.*
Ustedes *Ellos* *Ellas*	*tienen*	You guys, They **have**	*Ellos tienen mucho dinero.*
Nosotros *Nosotras*	*tenemos*	We **have**	*Tenemos un perro negro.*

Más about *tener*

Check this out! Besides meaning "to have," the verb *"tener"*
can also be used in these situations:

Tengo la culpa.	I'm at fault.
Tengo razón.	I'm right.
Tengo hambre.	I'm hungry.
Tengo frío.	I'm cold.
Tengo sed.	I'm thirsty.
Tengo calor.	I'm hot.
Tengo miedo.	I'm scared.
Tengo sueño.	I'm sleepy.
Tengo suerte.	I'm in luck.
Tengo 18 años.	I'm 18 years old.

 See how *tengo*
and *tiene*
are great for
requests and chit-chat.
¿Tiene usted dinero?
Do you have money?
Sí, tengo diez dólares.
Yes, I have ten dollars.

 **QUICK TIPS**

- *Tienes* goes with
  tú (informal you):
  *¿Cuántos años tienes
  tú, amigo?*
- Notice how these make
  great "one-liners":
  Tenemos miedo.
  We're scared.
  ¿Tiene frío?
  Are you cold?
  Tienen hambre.
  They're hungry.

¿Qué estás haciendo? (What Are You Doing?)

Verbs in Spanish are usually learned in a predictable order. First, the commands are picked up along with the forms of **ser**, **estar**, and **tener**. Then come the action words referring to "now!" (I call this the "-ing" or **-ndo** form.) It's the easiest form to remember and to use. All that's needed is an **acción** word! To say "talking" for example, simply change **hablar** (talk) to **hablando**:

hablar → to talk
hablando → talking

BillTalks

77

¡Yo hablo español! Check the app for more on the "-ing" words in Spanish.

The **-ndo** replaces the **-r**. All Spanish action words end in **-r**, so the **-ndo** or -ing form **es muy simple**! Start with the **-ar** verbs, because most infinitives end that way:

trabajar	**trabajando**
work	working
comprar	**comprando**
buy	buying
manejar	**manejando**
drive	driving

And here's how they work. Just add the forms of *estar*: ***ESTOY, ESTÁ, ESTÁN,*** or ***ESTAMOS***

> ***Estamos trabajando en el garaje.***
> We're working in the garage.

CAREFUL! Some *acción* words end in *-er* or *-ir*, so you have to change the ending to *-iendo* instead of *-ando*:

comer	***comiendo***
eat	eating

escribir	***escribiendo***
write	writing

> ***Estoy comiendo con mi familia.***
> I'm eating with my family.

QUICK TIPS

Relax! All you need to remember is to drop the *-ar, -er, -ir* and add either *-ando* or *-iendo*. And to "complete" your message, just put the *estar* words in front: "Maria is working." becomes ***María está trabajando.***

BillTalks

78   *¡Yo hablo español!*
Check the app for
more on the "-ing"
words in Spanish.

Onward with "-*ndo*"

The key to real fluency is to acquire as many ***acción*** words
as possible. Try "fooling around" with these words. First,
"-ing" 'em with -***ando*** or -***iendo***! Then use them to make
statements.

correr (run)
Ellos están corriendo.
They're running.

caminar (walk)
Estoy caminando.
I'm walking.

salir (leave)
El tren está saliendo.
The train is leaving.

QUICK TIPS

- Many action words
  are ***muy*** easy to
  remember.
  plantar   plant
  visitar   visit
  controlar   control
- And some are easier to
  learn combined with
  other words:
  marcar el número
  dial the number
  llamar por teléfono
  call by phone
  mirar televisión
  watch TV
- Be careful! A few
  action words are not
  what they seem!
  pretender
  to court someone
  embarazar
  to impregnate
- And a few of these
  words change a little
  when you add -***ndo***.
  leer (read) becomes
  leyendo (reading)
  dormir (sleep)
  becomes ***durmiendo***
  (sleeping)
  decir (say) becomes
  diciendo (saying)

abrir	open	*Jorge está abriendo la puerta.*
aprender	learn	
beber	drink	
besar	kiss	
cerrar	close	
empujar	push	
jalar	pull	
jugar	play	
lavar	wash	
limpiar	clean	
llegar	arrive	
llevar	carry	
llorar	cry	
mostrar	show	
pagar	pay	
parar	stop	
poner	put	
tirar	throw	
vender	sell	
viajar	travel	
volver	return	

When adding the "*-ndo*-ing," are you putting *estoy*, *está*, *están*, and *estamos* in front?

Ready, Set, . . .

At this stage of the guidebook, most of you have already started to race forward, constantly in search of *más palabras de acción*. You have found that knowing how to use the *-ndo* form changes everything. After jabbering a couple of *acciones*, along with some *vocabulario básico*, you have begun to feel like a native speaker. However, before you volunteer as a tour guide, let's first take a look at a few more secrets to understanding those action words!

Beyond -*ndo*

There's no way that beginning Spanish-speakers can pick up all the different action word forms right away. However, after the -*ndo's*, it is possible to shortcut your way through some of the other grammar junk.

Here is a **grupo** of goodies that will help! Put these phrases in front of the "infinitives," which are those basic verbs ending in -*ar*, -*er*, or -*ir*:

Me gusta (I like) . . .　　　　*Me gusta jugar.*

Hágame el favor de (Please) . . .　　*Hágame el favor de trabajar.*

Tengo que (I have to) . . .　_____

Debo (I should) . . .　_____

Prefiero (I prefer to) . . .　_____

Necesito (I need to) . . .　_____

Puedo (I can) . . .　_____

Deseo (I wish to) . . .　_____

Quiero (I want to) . . .　_____

Quisiera (I'd like to) . . .　_____

"SE"

A small number of *palabras de acción* have *se* attached. Don't get excited! It usually means that the action is one that we do to ourselves. Here's how they work.

lavar is "to wash." ***Ella está lavando el carro.*** (She is washing the car.)

lavarse means "to wash oneself." To *-ndo*, say *lavándose* (washing oneself).

Add *estar* and it's ***Ella está lavándose.*** (She's washing herself).

Check out some *más*! Can you guess how it's done?

acostarse	to lie down
Nosotros estamos acostándonos.	We're lying down.
bañarse	to bathe oneself
Ella está bañándose.	She's taking a bath.
cepillarse	to brush one's hair
Yo estoy cepillándome.	I'm brushing my hair.
levantarse	to raise oneself up
Yo estoy levantándome.	I'm getting up.
peinarse	to comb one's hair
Juan está peinándose.	John's combing his hair.
sentarse	to sit down
Ellos están sentándose.	They're sitting down.

CHOOSE 'n' USE!

¿Quién está . . .?	Who is . . . (bathing, standing, etc.)?
Estoy . . . ahora mismo.	I am . . . (lying down, etc.) right now.
Estamos . . . y . . .	We are . . . (combing) and . . . (brushing our hair).

This is not easy. Even native Spanish speakers sometimes have problems with these little devils! But don't let them bother you. For now, just be aware of their general meaning and importance.

lo, la, le, les, me, nos

Understanding these little pieces of Spanish is easier than using them correctly. So for now, here's what they usually mean when used with action words!

lo, la	it	**Estoy comprándolo.**	I'm buying it.
le	to you, him, her	**Dígale.**	Tell him.
les	to you guys, them	**Dígales.**	Tell them.
me	to me	**Dígame.**	Tell me.
nos	to us	**Díganos.**	Tell us.

The "little words" are everywhere in normal conversation:

Me lo dijo.	He told it to me.
Lo tengo.	I have it.
Nos la explica.	He explains it to us.
Escríbale.	Write to him.
No les hablo.	I don't talk to them.

And notice how they usually require the Reversal Rule!

La	**La estoy limpiando.**	I am cleaning it.
Lo	**Juan lo está haciendo.**	Juan is doing it.
Le	**Le están escribiendo.**	They are writing to you (or him, her).
Les	**Les estamos diciendo.**	We are telling them.
Me	**Sandra me está besando.**	Sandra is kissing me.
Nos	**Ella nos está enseñando.**	She is teaching us.

QUICK TIPS

- Some action words in the *se* category also change when you add *-ndo*!
- Let's face it, *se* is strange and needs more explanation. You might even hear *se* used in other ways. But don't let that slow you down! There are too few *se* actions to worry about.
- You'll also hear *te*, which is informal for saying "to you" (*¡Te amo!* I love you!).
- Go online and research both "*se*" and "object pronouns in Spanish" if you need more info.

Still *más palabras de acción*

Here are more of those practical, everyday action words (infinitives) that you really can use all the time!

adivinar	guess	**¿Puede adivinar mi nombre?**		
amar	love	*juntar*	join
apostar	bet	*montar*	ride
aprovechar	take advantage	*nadar*	swim
arreglar	arrange	*odiar*	hate
asistir	attend	*olvidar*	forget
bailar	dance	*perder*	lose
buscar	look for	*pesar*	weigh
cantar	sing	*pescar*	fish
celebrar	celebrate	*prestar*	lend
cocinar	cook	*probar*	try
contestar	answer	*quebrar*	break
cortar	cut	*quitar*	take away
dar	give	*recibir*	receive
desarrollar	develop	*renunciar*	quit
descansar	rest	*reparar*	fix
desear	wish	*sobrevivir*	survive
disfrutar	enjoy	*soñar*	dream
empezar	begin	*subir*	climb
encontrar	find	*terminar*	finish
escuchar	listen	*tocar*	touch
evitar	avoid	*traducir*	translate
gastar	spend	*usar*	to use
gritar	yell	*viajar*	to travel
jugar	play	*volar*	to fly

Don't forget: *-er, -ir > -iendo* and *-ar > -ando*

CHOOSE 'n' USE!

Mi amigo está . . .

My friend is . . . (yelling, fishing, etc.).

Los niños están . . .

The children are . . . (guessing, etc.).

Yo estoy . . . mucho.

I am . . . (translating, etc.) a lot.

Nosotros no estamos . . .

We are not . . . (flying, riding, etc.).

¿Ustedes están . . .?

Are you guys . . . (listening, etc.)?

El Sr. Gómez está . . . y . . .

Mr. Gomez is . . . (swimming, etc.) and . . . (climbing, etc.).

Las acciones locas

No doubt you have some questions about a few action words that don't seem to perform like the others. I call them "*las locas*" (the "crazies"). Let's take a look at a few of my favorites:

Ir (to go)

What's *fantástico* about *ir* is that it tells . . .

. . . where you're "going to" and

. . . what you're "going to" do later.

Learn these words:

Voy a (I'm "going to") . . . *San Francisco.*

Va a (You're, He's, She's "going to") . . . *mi casa.*

Van a (You guys, They are "going to") . . . *bailar.*

Vamos a (We're "going to") . . . *comer.*

Did you notice? Apply *ir* a to talk about the "future"!

¡Usted va a hablar español!
You're going to speak Spanish!

¡Victoria va a cocinar mañana!
Victoria's going to cook tomorrow!

¡Nosotros vamos a salir luego!
We're gonna go out later!

 IR + A is kind of a "Future Tense," so you can use the formula to talk about what you're "gonna do" later. Another important "Future Tense" is explained on page 232 in the back of the book.

Saber and conocer (To know)

Saber and **conocer** both mean to know, but here's how they differ:

saber (*sé, sabe, saben, sabemos*) means "to know something."

conocer (*conozco, conoce, conocen, conocemos*) means "to know someone."

Yo sé mucho español.	I know a lot of Spanish.
Yo conozco a muchas personas.	I know a lot of people.

sé, conozco I know

sabe, conoce you, he, she knows

saben, conocen they, you guys know

sabemos, conocemos we know

¿Qué pasó?
What Happened?

Unfortunately, telling someone about previous events in Spanish can be done several ways, depending upon your meaning. These are learned gradually when exposed consistently to lots of ***español***. So, for the ***momento***, let's view a few common "past" words that can help you ASAP.

Dijo	said (you, he, she)	***¿Qué dijo?***
Fue	went (you, he, she)	***¿Adónde fue?***
Comí	ate (I)	***¡Comí tres tacos!***
Tenía	used to have (I, you, he, she)	***Tenía problemas con el wi-fi.***
Iba	was going (I, he, she); were going (you)	***Iba a mirar la tele visión.***

There are many more – check out the preterit tense in Appendix A: Basic Verb Tenses.

QUICK TIPS

- *"Estaba"* goes great with the *-ndo*'s. Also, there are only three "estaba" words to recall; not four!
- Beware! There are other "was" words. Believe me, this "was" word will get you going. You can finally start talking about the past:
  Ella estaba aquí ayer.   She was here yesterday.
  Estábamos trabajando anoche. We were working last night.
  Yo no estaba en casa. I wasn't home.
  ¿Estaban jugando ellos? Were they playing?

Estaba

Estaba is also used to talk about past action.
¿Qué estaba haciendo? What were you doing?

Try these words to answer:

Yo	Usted	Ella, Él	Ellos, Ustedes	Nosotros
estaba	estaba	estaba	estaban	estábamos
I was	You were	She was, He was	They were, You guys were	We were

There are tons of other examples, and are explained in some detail at the back of this book. Of course, you can always search online for the **PAST TENSE IN SPANISH** if you want to learn more.

CHOOSE 'n' USE!

¿Qué dijo . . .?	What did . . . say? (Mary, Tom, etc.)?
Comí en . . .	I ate at (the) . . . (restaurant, house, etc.).
No estaban . . .	They weren't . . . (working, eating, etc.).
Él no tenía . . .	He didn't have the . . . (name, number, etc.).
Fue a . . .	You, He, She went to . . . (Japan, Europe, etc.).

Unos consejos (Some Advice)

Bueno, before we "stop the action," here's some helpful "inside info" on Spanish ***acciones y actividades.***

1 The world of "Spanish slang" has also produced action words that can be heard daily, particularly in those areas of the United States where lots of both Spanish and English are spoken. Try some! (Many sound the same in English.) And of course, make sure you understand what you're saying. You'll need to use your best judgment!

2 Read ***español***. This is perhaps one of the best ways to learn the various action word forms (tenses). You'll soon be picking up and using stuff that used to take the rest of us years to learn!

3 Notice that action words in ***español*** have the same form for "we"! No matter what you're trying to say, the ***nosotros*** (we) ending is *-**mos***.

	somos.	We are.
Nosotros	***bailamos***.	We dance.
	comimos.	We ate.

4 Similarly, the "they" and "you guys" ending is also easy to remember. Listen for the final "***n***":

	son.	They or you guys are.
Ellos or ***ustedes***	***bailan***.	They or you guys dance.
	comieron.	They or you guys ate.

5 These are only a couple of ***muchos*** patterns that remain consistent among Spanish action words. So pay attention! You are bound to discover many more.

"Mente" at the end!

There's a unique set of words in Spanish that really go *bien* with the *palabras de acción*. They tell "how we do things." What's nice is they all end in -*mente*. (Notice how much they look like *inglés*!)

brevemente	briefly
correctamente	correctly
efectivamente	effectively
inmediatamente	immediately
perfectamente	perfectly
rápidamente	rapidly
sinceramente	sincerely
usualmente	usually

Read aloud:

Juan está trabajando rápidamente.
Juan's working rapidly.

Estoy hablando sinceramente.
I'm talking sincerely.

Estamos jugando perfectamente.
We're playing perfectly.

¿PUEDE RECORDARLO?
(Can You Remember It?)

☑ Give a few commands in Spanish.

☑ Make three different statements using the word *estoy*.

☑ Make three different statements using the word *soy*.

☑ Ask a question using the word *tiene*.

☑ Make a statement using the word *hablando*.

☑ Name five basic verbs in Spanish.

☑ Make a statement using the word *estaba*.

☑ What does *perfectamente* mean?

8

CHAPTER *OCHO*

Los detalles

(Details)

Tell Me When!

QUICK TIPS

- As with everything else, keep your eyes and ears open for *más*!
- *Tiempo* refers to "time in general," though in some cases, *tiempo* can mean "weather." *La hora* is clock time, and to say "one time," it's *una vez*.
- These "time" *palabras* are extremely valuable when used with your action words: *¡Siempre hablo español, cada día y todo el tiempo!*

We've become familiar with some of these "when" words already. But now – with our knowledge of *¿Cuándo?* (and some *palabras básicas*) – it's time to present the most popular words and phrases referring to time. Recognize any of these one-liners?

ahora	now, today, nowadays	*Hace calor ahora.*
ahorita, ahora mismo	right now	
a la madrugada	at dawn	
a la puesta del sol	at sunset	
anoche	last night	
anteayer	the day before yesterday	
antes	before	
apenas	just	
a veces	sometimes	
ayer	yesterday	
cada día	each day	
casi nunca	seldom	
después	afterward	
entonces	then	
esta noche	tonight	
hace mucho tiempo	a long time ago	
hasta	until	
hoy	today	
luego	later	
mañana	tomorrow	
mañana por la mañana	tomorrow morning	

el mes pasado	last month
muchas veces	lots of times
nunca	never
pasado mañana	the day after tomorrow
pronto	soon
la próxima semana	next week
el próximo mes	next month
la semana pasada	last week
siempre	always
tarde	late
temprano	early
todavía	yet
todo el tiempo	all the time
todos los días	every day
una vez	once
un momento	a moment
un rato	awhile
ya	already

CHOOSE 'n' USE!

Trabajo . . .	I work . . . (today, always, etc.).
Estoy trabajando . . .	I'm working . . . (right now, late, etc.).
Estaba trabajando . . .	I was working . . . (yesterday, then, etc.).
He trabajado . . .	I've worked . . . (before, every day, etc.).
Voy a trabajar . . .	I'm going to work . . . (tomorrow, next month, etc.).

Tell Me Where!

Many "location" words were introduced earlier. The subsequent phrases and words allow us to express exactly where something (or someone) is located.

With these little beauties, you can answer almost any **¿Dónde?** question. They're OK alone, but they're better in sentences. (You'd be "lost" without them.)

abajo   down   ***Estoy mirando abajo.***

adentro, dentro de	inside	**debajo de**	under
		desde	from
afuera, fuera de	outside	**detrás de**	behind
		en	in, on, at
al fondo de	at the bottom	**encima de**	above
al lado de	next to	**enfrente de**	in front of
a lo largo de	along	**entre**	between
alrededor de	around	**hacia**	towards
arriba de	up	**lejos de**	far from
cerca de	near	**sobre**	over
contra	against		

CHOOSE 'n' USE!

Voy a ponerlo . . . los paquetes.   I'm going to put it . . . (inside, above, etc.) the packages.

La oficina está . . . las tiendas.   The office is . . . (near, next to, etc.) the stores.

El perrito está corriendo . . . ellos.   The puppy is running . . . (toward, between, etc.) them.

Super "where" words!

por cualquier lado
anywhere

por algún lugar
somewhere

por ningún lado
nowhere

por todas partes
everywhere

The Wimpy Wonder Words

Cosas buenas often come in small packages, and that's true for Spanish, too! Study this handful of tiny words that are heard often, because of their extreme importance. Combine one word from each list:

en (in, on, at) . . .	**mí** (me)	**Piense en mí.**
de (from, of) . . .	**usted** (you)	**El dinero es de usted.**
a (to) . . .	**él** (him)	**Visitamos a él.**
para (for, in order to) . . .	**ella** (her)	**Es para ella.**
por (by, through) . . .	**ellos, ellas** (them)	**Pase por ellos.**
	ustedes (you guys)	
	nosotros, nosotras (us)	
	_____ (name of person, place, or thing)	

And watch for these "Wee Wonders"!

sin	without	**Estoy sin wifi.**
con	with	**Estoy con wifi.**

However, check the changes:

conmigo	with me
consigo	with you, him, her, them
contigo	with you (between friends, family)

See how these "who" words change slightly when followed by the "where" words.

BillTalks

79

¡Yo hablo español! Check the app for more on making phrases with **a, de, con,** and **sin**.

QUICK TIP

Spanish has two contractions: **a** (to) and **de** (of, from) always mesh with **el** (the):

del   **Soy del centro.**
I'm from downtown.

al   **Voy al lago.**
I'm going to the lake.

Get It Together – Part II

No more fooling around. It's time for the amateurs to step aside. This stuff is for the "pros" only!

Now that action words have been introduced, let's see what they look like when we combine them with all the other stuff. The key is to continue building strings of words – much like we do in English – but without fear of making mistakes! Here's a simple formula:

La persona + La acción + Lugar + Tiempo = ¡Mucho español!
   (person)   (action)   (place)   (time)

Roberto está trabajando en la tienda ahorita.
Robert is working in the store right now.

To elaborate, add **_descripción_** and detail!

Mi amigo Roberto está trabajando en la tienda nueva hoy con María.
My friend Robert is working at the new store today with María.

Mis amigos americanos, Roberto y María, no están trabajando mucho en la tienda nueva, porque ellos tienen clases todos los días.
My American friends, Robert and María, aren't working a lot at the new store, because they have classes every day.

Now, change the subject. Try mixing the order of your phrases.

Tengo problemas con el brazo y el sábado no puedo jugar en el parque con las otras muchachas.
I have problems with my arm, and I can't play at the park with the other girls on Saturday.

Or, how about forming a **_pregunta_**?

¿Su hermana va a la tienda y va a comprar la comida para la cena y también dulces para los niños?
Is your sister going to the store and is she going to buy food for dinner and also candy for the kids?

There isn't a thing you can't talk about!

Un elefante gordo estaba bañándose en el río ayer y estaba comiendo las plantas debajo del agua.
A fat elephant was bathing in the river yesterday and was eating the plants under the water.

When you get **bueno** at combining your Spanish words, the **El** and **La** Business, the Reversal Rule and the Once-and-for-All Rule will be applied without effort – automatically! Just remember, the more you "babble," the better you'll be!

Also, lengthen those commands! Check back on the **mandatos** (pages 112–114), and "add on" a few **palabras**:

¡Hable!   Speak!

¡Hable con Tina!   Speak with Tina!

. . . add some more:

¡Hable con Tina en la oficina!   Speak with Tina in the office!

And don't forget to combine two or more commands with the little linkers – **de, a, para, sin,** and **con**:

¡Vaya a la escuela y hable con Tina en la oficina!
Go to school and speak with Tina in the office!

QUICK TIP

A "change" in the word order does not usually affect the meaning of the message!
When you need to stop and "collect your thoughts," why not mutter a word, such as *¡Un momento!* (One moment!).

Please say *por favor*.

BillTalks

80

¡Yo hablo español! Check the app for a quiz to test what you have learned.

RSVP

As your strings of *palabras* get longer you'll need techniques to help you over any minor hurdles that may impede communication. Instead of walking away from a good conversation, try the **RSVP** (**R**epeat, **S**lur, **V**isualize, **P**ause) method of keeping things going. RSVP works, so master it *lo más pronto posible* (as soon as possible).

Repeat it!

Repeating what you hear is still one of the best ways to acquire language while conversing. Hearing and saying (instead of doing nothing at all) new words more than once, make comprehension and speech that much easier. *¿Hay mucho tráfico hoy? ¡Sí, hay mucho tráfico hoy!*

Slur it!

As ridiculous as it may seem, while you're learning Spanish, one very safe way to stay in a conversation is to slur and mumble those words, or parts of words, that you're not very sure of. Using English, Spanglish, and even "creating" your own Spanish words are also very effective ways to reduce your "drop-out" rate.

Visualize it!

When listening or speaking, just picture the unfamiliar words in their written form! Since Spanish is always pronounced exactly like it is spelled, comprehension is easy. Try it and you'll SEE! And are you still using the other "visualization" technique? Keep playing those word-picture association games. Here are two of my favorites:

libro (book) looks like library

cuartos (rooms) looks like quarters

P-a-u-s-e it!

For those moments of silence when you're desperately trying to recall words and form a response, try interjecting these lifesavers!

A ver . . .	Let's see . . .
Este . . .	Uh . . .
O sea . . .	What I mean is . . .
Bueno . . .	OK . . .
Es decir . . .	That is to say . . .
Pues . . .	Well . . .

BillTalks

¡Yo hablo español! Check the app for more on the RSVP techniques.

QUICK TIP

Spanish mutterings are like those in English, so put two or three in a row! Well . . . let's see . . . OK! *Pues . . . a ver . . . ¡bueno!*

Not much more to fluency now!

¿PUEDE RECORDARLO?
(Can You Remember It?)

☑ Name five words that tell "when" something takes place.

☑ Name five words that tell "where" something takes place.

☑ Use these little words in a sentence:

a _____

en _____

para _____

☑ What does RSVP stand for in this guidebook?

9

CHAPTER *NUEVE*
Más detalles
(More Details)

¿*Quiere jugar?* (Wanna Play?)

Americans love sports and recreation. And so do many Spanish speakers worldwide. For the Latin American, soccer is the king of sports. (They call it *fútbol*.) El *béisbol* is popular as well; in fact, if you need "listening practice," many ball games are broadcasted on the Internet, cable TV, and radio in both English and Spanish. As for individual hobbies (*pasatiempos*) in Latin America, they vary from one person to the next, just as they do in the United States. So, which of the following Spanish words might be helpful to you in your spare time?

Keep in mind, many sound like *inglés!*

Los deportes (Sports)

Me gusta mucho ____.	I really like____.
el automovilismo	auto racing
el básquetbol, el baloncesto	basketball
el béisbol	baseball
el boliche	bowling
el boxeo	boxing
el ciclismo	biking
el fisiculturismo	bodybuilding
el fútbol	soccer
el fútbol americano	football
la gimnasia	gymnastics
el motocliclismo	motocross
la natación	swimming
el sóftbol	softball
el tenis	tennis
el vóleibol	volleyball

Guess their meanings!

Hockey, surf, golf, bádminton, ráquetbol, snowboard, rodeo, yoga, ping-pong, skateboarding, lacrosse, paddleboard, water polo

And here are some action words in the "workout" category:

ir al gimnasio	to go to the gym
levantar pesas	to lift weights
hacer ejercicio	to do exercise

CHOOSE 'n' USE!

¿Le gusta . . . o . . .?	Do you like . . . (baseball, etc.) or . . . (football, etc.)?
No sé mucho de . . .	I don't know much about . . . (fishing, auto racing, etc.).
. . . es excelente para su salud.	. . . (Tennis, Swimming, etc.) is great for your health.
Necesitamos . . .	We need the . . . (volleyball, softball, etc.).

How about these "winners"!

¿Juega Ud. a . . .?	Do you play . . .?
¿Quién ganó?	Who won?
¿Cuántos tantos?	What's the score?
¿Quién perdió?	Who lost?
¿Ellos empataron?	Are they tied?

¿Dónde está_____?	**Where's the ____?**
el anfiteatro	arena
el atleta	athlete
el bate	bat
el campeonato	championship
el campo	field
la canasta	basket
la cancha	court
el entrenador	coach
el equipo	team

el estadio	stadium
el fanático	fan
el guante	mitt
el juego	game
la linea	line
el partido	match
la pelota or *la bola*	ball
la piscina	pool
la práctica	practice
la raqueta	racket
la red	net
el uniforme	uniform

Mi pasatiempo favorito (My Favorite Hobby)

Hablamos de____.	Let's talk about____.
la actuación	acting
las apuestas en línea	online betting
las artes marciales	martial arts
la artesanía	handicrafts
la astronomía	astronomy
el baile	dancing
el canto	singing
los deportes virtuales	virtual sports
el dibujo	drawing
la escritura	writing
la escultura	sculpture
la fotografía	photography
la jardinería	gardening
los juegos de mesa	board games
la lectura	reading

la pintura	painting
el tejido de punto	knitting
los videojuegos	video games

Me gusta____.	**I like ____.**
cocinar	to cook
coleccionar	to collect things
coser	to sew
cuidar a las mascotas	to take care of pets
escuchar música	to listen to music
estudiar	to study
hacer tareas del hogar	to do household chores
hornear	to bake
ir a conciertos	to go to concerts
ir al cine	to go to the movies
ir al teatro	to go to the theater
ir de compras	to go shopping
ir de excursión	to take trips
jugar a las cartas	to play cards
jugar al billar	to shoot pool
mirar videos	to watch videos
pasar tiempo con la familia	to spend time with family
pasar un rato con los amigos	to hang out with friends
relajar	to relax
salir a comer	to go out to eat
tocar algún instrumento	to play an instrument
trabajar como voluntario	to do volunteer work
usar la computadora	to use the computer
ver la tele	to watch TV
ver partidos	to watch sports
viajar a otros países	to travel to other countries

¿Quiere____?	**Do you want____?**
acampar	to camp
bucear	to go scuba diving
dar una caminata	to hike
escalar montañas	to climb mountains
esquiar	to ski
ir de caza	to go hunting
montar a caballo	to ride on horseback
navegar	to sail
pasear	to take a walk
pasear en barco	to go boating
patinar	to skate
pescar	to fish
trotar	to jog

Jugar con los juguetes (Play with Toys)

Besides *los juegos* (games), we all grow up *jugando con* (playing with) toys. Kids of all ages will want to know the Spanish words for some of the common play *cosas*!

*Mire*_____	**Look at (the)**_____
la bicicleta	bike
el carrito de carrera	race car
la casa de muñecas	dollhouse
el control remoto	remote control
los cubos	blocks
el dron	drone
la espada de juguete	play sword
la figura de acción	action toy
la muñeca	doll
los patines	skates
la patineta	skateboard
la pelota	ball
el peluche	stuffed animal
el reloj inteligente	smart watch
el robot	robot
el rompecabezas	puzzle
el triciclo	tricycle
el trineo	sled

Los juegos de mesa (Board Games)

Jugamos_____.	Let's play_____.
ajedrez	chess
dados	dice
dominó	dominoes
juego de damas	checkers
Monopolio	Monopoly
naipes	cards
rompecabezas	puzzles

Es____.	It's____.
colecccionable	collectable
digital	digital
educativo	educational
electrónico	electronic
incluido	included
interactivo	interactive
intercambiable	interchangeable
movible	moveable
portátil	portable
recargable	rechargeable
transformable	transformable
virtual	virtual

¡La fiesta! (Party!)

No tenemos_____.　　**We don't have (the)_____.**

las bebidas	drinks
los chistes	jokes
la comida	food
las decoraciones	decorations
los disfraces	costumes
el DJ	disk jockey
los fuegos artificiales	fireworks
los globos	balloons
el papel de regalo	gift wrapping
los regalos	gifts
los trucos de magia	magic tricks

And for the little ones?

Necesita_____.　　**He/She needs the_____.**

el biberón	baby's bottle
el chupete	pacifier
los colores/crayones	crayons
los dibujos animados	cartoons
la mantita	blanket
los marcadores	markers

The word for "fun" is "*la diversión*." but the word "funny" is "*chistoso*."

QUICK TIPS

- For a "toy" object: *tren de juguete* (toy train); *soldado de juguete* (toy soldier); *celular de juguete* (toy phone).
- Always focus on the *inglés*: *el dinosaurio, el unicornio, el dragón*.
- In fact, use English: *los Legos, la Barbie, los Hot Wheels, la Nintendo, el Nerf*, etc.
- You may need to mention these words as well: *la app* (application), *los accesorios* (accessories), *las pilas* (batteries).

¡Siga jugando! (Keep Playing!)

A theatrical play in Spanish has nothing to do with the action word "play." It is an **obra de teatro** (a theatrical work). Yet, if **el teatro** is your thing, maybe you can use these words below:

la acción	action	**La escena tiene mucha acción.**
el ceño	frown	
la comedia	comedy	
la escena	scene	
el escenario	stage	
el horror	horror	
las lágrimas	tears	
el misterio	mystery	
el romance	romance	
la risa	laughter	
la sonrisa	smile	
la tragedia	tragedy	

To play a musical instrument requires *tocar* (to touch) instead of *jugar*. Check out how *tocar* sounds when combined with these popular *instrumentos musicales* (musical instruments):

¿*Toca usted*____?	**Do you play the**____?
el arpa	harp
la armónica	harmonica
el clarinete	clarinet
la flauta	flute
la guitarra	guitar
el órgano	organ
el piano	piano
el saxofón	saxophone
el tambor	drum
el trombón	trombone
la trompeta	trumpet
la viola	viola
el violín	violin

Here are more words that look a lot like *inglés*!

CHOOSE 'n' USE!

Mi hijo quiere . . .	My kid wants . . . (a guitar, etc.).
Tengo . . . *y* . . .	I have . . . (a piano, etc.) and . . . (a violin, etc.).
¿*Dónde puedo comprar* . . .?	Where can I buy . . . (a clarinet, etc.)?

Travel Treats!

We've already covered a few helpful areas for the traveler, such as transportation, shopping, and restaurant talk. The following collection of words, however, includes the best of Spanish *palabras* and *frases*, which will assist not only the experienced *turista*, but the occasional vacationer as well: Let's begin with the "lifesavers":

¿A qué distancia?	How far?
¿Cuál autobús?	Which bus?
¿Cuál calle?	Which street?
¿Cuánto tiempo?	How much time?
¿Está incluido(a)?	Is it included?
¿Está listo(a)?	Is it ready?
¿Está ocupado(a)?	Is it taken?
¿Hay agua potable?	Is there drinking water?
¿Puede ayudarme?	Can you help me?
¿Puede recomendar uno(a)?	Can you recommend one?
¿Puedo pagar con esto?	Can I pay with this?
¿Puede repararlo(a)?	Can you fix it?
¿Puedo tener cambio?	Can I have change?

And don't leave home without . . .

Busco_____.	**I'm looking for_____.**
el aeropuerto the airport	***Estoy buscando el aeropuerto.***
el banco	the bank
el baño	the restroom
el camino a . . .	the road to . . .
la carretera de peaje	the toll road
el centro	downtown
el correo	the post office
el cruce de peatones	the crosswalk
la entrada	the entrance
la estación	the station
el estacionamiento	the parking
el hospital	the hospital
el hotel	the hotel
el mapa	the map
el mercado	the market
la parada de autobús	the bus stop
el restaurante	the restaurant
la salida	the exit
el semáforo	the traffic light
la señal	the road sign
el sitio de web	the website
la tienda	the store

Use your time-telling skills!
¿Qué día es hoy? What day is today?
¿A qué hora? At what time?

Más personas muy necesarias:

Es____.	He/She is the____.
el/la botones	bellhop
el/la chofer	driver
el/la conserje	concierge
el/la criado(a)	maid
el/la dueño(a)	owner
el/la gerente(a)	manager
el/la guardia	security guard
el/la guía	guide
el/la mesero(a)	waiter/waitress

Here's a mixed bag of super sayings. Follow the pattern as you fill in the words below:

Quiero (I want)____.

Necesito (I need)____.

Quisiera (I'd like)____.

darle propina	to give you a tip	*Quiero darle propina.*
hacer reservaciones	to make reservations	*Necesito hacer reservaciones.*
cargarlo(a)	to charge it	*Quisiera cargarlo.*
pagarlo(a)	to pay it	
cambiarlo(a)	to exchange it	
ordenar	to order	
un boleto	a ticket	
la contraseña	the password	
el sitio de web	website	
el enlace	link	
la ubicación	the location	
la llave	the key	
un taxi	a taxi	

más toallas	more towels
una habitación	a room
más hielo	more ice
una bebida	a drink
la cuenta	the bill
un corte de pelo	a haircut
cancelarlo(a)	cancel it
una suite	a suite
el ascensor	the elevator
el servicio de cuarto	room service
el recibo	the receipt
hacer un recorrido	to take a tour
las escaleras	the stairs
la piscina	the pool
el gimnasio	the gym
un café	a coffee shop

Pack these words away, too!

la aduana	customs	*¿Dónde esta la aduana?*
la agencia de viajes	travel agency	
los aparatos electrónicos	electronic devices	
el boleto de ida y vuelta	round-trip ticket	
el equipaje	luggage	
las maletas	suitcases	
el pasaporte	passport	
los puntos de interés	points of interest	
el seguro	insurance	
la seguridad	security (TSA)	
la tarjeta de embarque	boarding pass	
la visa	visa	

El carro (The Car)

Las partes del vehículo (Auto Parts)

el asiento	seat	*El asiento está sucio.*
la batería	battery	
el capó	hood	
el cinturón de seguridad	seat belt	
el espejo	mirror	
los frenos	brakes	
la guantera	glove box	
el guardabarros	bumper	
el limpiaparabrisas	wipers	
las luces delanteras	headlights	
el maletero	trunk	
el motor	engine	
el parabrisas	windshield	
la placa	license plate	
la puerta	door	
el radiador	radiator	
el silenciador	muffler	
el techo	roof	
la ventanilla	car window	
el volante	steering wheel	

Driving does have its setbacks:

¡Estamos sin gasolina!	We're out of gas!
¡Tengo una llanta desinflada!	I have a flat tire!
¡Estamos perdidos!	We're lost!
No funciona.	It doesn't work.
¡Hay mucho tráfico!	There's a lot of traffic!

Es____.	It's (the)____.
el aceite	oil Es el aceite.
el agua	water
el enchufe	plug
el filtro	filter
la gasolina	gas
el líquido	fluid
la manguera	hose
el sensor	sensor

¡La pesca! (Fishing!)

This is my favorite way to relax – and practice my Spanish at the same time!

Tengo____.	I have (the)____.
el anzuelo	hook
el bote	boat
la caña de pescar	rod
el carrete	reel
el cordel	line
el nudo	knot
el salvavidas	life jacket

Voy a____.	I'm going____.
lanzar	to cast
navegar	to sail
remar	to row

Mire____.	Look at the____.
la bahía	bay
la costa	coast
la isla	island
el mar	sea
la marea	tide
las olas	waves
la orilla	shore

La farmacia (The Pharmacy)

Now, sample this selection! You might need them along the way:

Voy a comprar____.	**I'm going to buy the___.**
el alfiler	pin *Voy a comprar el alfiler.*
la cerradura	lock
las estampillas	stamps
los fósforos	matches
el hilo	thread
la liga	rubber band
el periódico	newspaper
la revista	magazine
el sobre	envelope

And don't forget those toiletries!

¿Vas a comprar_____?	**Are you going to buy_____?**
el cepillo	hair brush *¿Vas a comprar el cepillo?*
el cepillo de dientes	toothbrush
el champú	shampoo
el cortaúñas	nail clippers
el desodorante	deodorant
el enjuague	conditioner
el jabón	soap
el limpiador	cleanser
el maquillaje	makeup
la medicina	medicine
las navajas	razors
el papel higiénico	toilet paper
la pasta de dientes	toothpaste
el peine	comb
las pinzas	tweezers
las toallas de papel	paper towels

QUICK TIPS

Containers come in all shapes and sizes. Pack it up, travelers!

el frasco	flask
	¡Tengo el frasco de vino!
la bolsa	bag
la botella	bottle
la canasta	basket
la caja	box
la lata	can
la paquete	package
la tubo	tube

Find out the names for the currency and its rate of exchange before you travel abroad. Before you leave, practice pronouncing any words or phrases you'll need.

Survival Signs

In traveling, the key to success is awareness. So, keep your *ojos* open for these common *letreros* (signs) and you won't get lost (or cited)!

ABIERTO	Open	**AVISO**	Warning
CERRADO	Closed	**EMERGENCIA**	Emergency
ALTO	Stop	**CRUZ ROJA**	Red Cross
CEDA EL PASO	Yield	**EMPUJE**	Push
DESPACIO	Slow	**JALE**	Pull
DESVIACIÓN	Detour	**NO FUMAR**	No Smoking
DIRECCIÓN ÚNICA	One Way	**SANITARIOS**	Restrooms
ENTRADA	Entrance	**DAMAS**	Ladies
SALIDA	Exit	**CABALLEROS**	Gentlemen
MINUSVÁLIDOS	Handicapped	**SE ALQUILA**	For Rent
ESTACIONAMIENTO	Parking	**SE VENDE**	For Sale
VÍA EQUIVOCADA	Wrong Way		
ROTONDA	Traffic Circle		
DESCOMPUESTO	Out of Order		

Las medidas (Measurements)

No matter where you go, most measurements matter!

¿Cuántos/as_____?		**How many_____?**	
onzas	ounces	**yardas**	yardas
libras	pounds	**tazas**	cups
pulgadas	inches	**cuartos**	quarts
millas	miles	**galones**	gallons
pies	feet	**grados**	degrees

Study your conversions to metrics, too!

centímetros	centimeters
gramos	grams
litros	liters
metros	meters
milímetros	millimeters

el kilómetro = 5/8 mile

el kilogramo = 2.2 lbs.

0°C (Celsius) = 32°F

QUICK TIPS

If you like numbers, make up a list of your own *favoritas*:

fracción	fraction
medio	half
por ciento	per cent

¿*Cuál es*____?	What's the____?	
la temperatura	temperature	*¿Cuál es la temperatura?*
la altitud	height	
el diámetro	diameter	
la distancia	distance	
la longitud	length	
el peso	weight	
la profundidad	depth	
la velocidad	speed	

Try these on for size!

+	*más*	*5 + 5 cinco más cinco*
-	*menos*	_____
×	*por*	_____
÷	*dividido*	_____

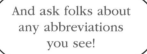

And ask folks about any abbreviations you see!

CHOOSE 'n' USE!

Primero vamos a buscar . . .	First, let's look for the . . . (passport, bellhop, etc.).
¿*Qué significa . . .?*	What does . . . (customs, for rent, etc.) mean?
Présteme . . .	Lend me the . . . (camera, key, etc.).

What's in a *Nombre*?

It's amazing how much influence Spanish has had over the years in many parts of the United States. Yet, we seldom stop to ponder the meaning of names of many of our cities, states, and landmarks. Some of them may surprise you.

Alamo	Poplar tree	*Rio Grande*	Large river
Amarillo	Yellow	*Sacramento*	Sacrament
Colorado	Red	*San Antonio*	Saint Anthony
El Paso	The pass		
Florida	Flowery	*San Diego*	Saint James
Las Vegas	The plains	*San Francisco*	Saint Francis
Los Angeles	The angels		
Montana	Mountain	*Santa Fe*	Holy Faith
Nevada	Snowfall	*Sierra*	Mountain range

Southwestern Specials

There's one part of the United States that's got *español* literally everywhere! Here are words that can be seen or heard throughout the Southwest:

agua	water	*palo*	stick, stump
arroyo	creek	*playa*	beach
costa	coast	*puerto*	port
lago	lake	*real*	royal
loma	hill	*santa* or *san*	saint
mar	sea	*valle*	valley
misión	mission	*vista*	view
monte	mountain		

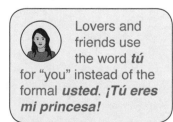

Lovers and friends use the word *tú* for "you" instead of the formal *usted*. ¡*Tú eres mi princesa!*

la avenida	avenue
el camino	road
la calle	street

¿Y su nombre?

And how about *los nombres de personas*? Obviously, those listed here are only a sample. Yours may or may not have an equivalent. (Ask around!)

QUICK TIPS

- Some proper names are written the same in both languages: David, Samuel, Daniel, Gloria, Linda, Virginia, Laura, etc.
- Some have "nicknames": Ignacio is "Nacho," Guillermo is "Memo," José is "Pepe."
- And add -ito for endearment; Juan becomes "Juanito."

Male Names

Al	*Alfredo*
Alex	*Alejandro*
Bob	*Roberto*
Charlie	*Carlos*
Eddie	*Eduardo*
Frank	*Francisco*
George	*Jorge*
Jim	*Jaime, Santiago*
Joe	*José*
John	*Juan*
Mark	*Marcos*
Mike	*Miguel*
Peter	*Pedro*
Rick	*Ricardo*
Steve	*Esteban*
Tim	*Timoteo*
Tom	*Tomás*
William	*Guillermo*

Female Names

Alice	*Alicia*
Ann	*Ana*
Barb	*Bárbara*
Carol	*Carolina*
Debbie	*Débora*
Helen	*Elena*
Jane	*Juanita*
Kathy	*Catalina*
Liz	*Isabel*
Marge	*Margarita*
Martha	*Marta*
Mary	*María*
Nancy	*Anita*
Rachel	*Raquel*
Sally	*Sara*
Susan	*Susana*

That's *Amor*

This guidebook would be incomplete without the presentation of the most significant Spanish "love lines." Romance is only a few *palabras* away.

Soy_____.	**I'm_____.**
casado(a)	married
divorciado(a)	divorced
separado(a)	separated
soltero(a)	single
viudo(a)	widowed

Love Lines

Estoy enamorado(a).	I'm in love.
Es una promesa.	It's a promise.
¿Te gustó?	Did you enjoy it?
Me divertí mucho.	I had a nice time.
¿Puedo verte más tarde?	Can I see you later?
¿Quieres casarte conmigo?	Will you marry me?
Te quiero muchísimo.	I love you so much.

¿Quisieras____?	**Would you like to____?**
bailar?	dance?
encontrarme allí?	meet me there?
dar un paseo?	take a walk?
platicar?	chat?
salir conmigo?	go out with me?

¿*Cómo es?* (What's He, or She, Like?)

Es____.   He's or She's____.

agradable	pleasant	*guapo(a)*	handsome
amable	kind	*honesto(a)*	honest
amistoso(a)	friendly	*responsable*	responsible
apasionado(a)	passionate	*romántico(a)*	romantic
aplicado(a)	studious	*sensible*	sensitive
celoso(a)	jealous	*simpático(a)*	nice
chistoso(a)	funny	*sincero(a)*	sincere
cruel	mean	*tímido(a)*	shy
educado(a)	well-mannered	*¡Besos!*	Kisses! XXXX
fiel	faithful	*¡Abrazos!*	Hugs! OOOO

More Nice Things to Say

Ellos son____.	They are____.	*Es mi____.*	He's/She's my____.
amantes	lovers	*chulo(a)*	cutie pie
socios	partners	*amor*	love
compañeros	companions	*corazón*	sweetheart
buenos amigos	good friends	*dulce*	sweetie
novios	boyfriend and girlfriend	*todo*	everything
recién casados	newlyweds	*tesoro*	treasure
una pareja	a couple	*vida*	love of my life
		querido(a)	darling
		precioso(a)	precious
		alma gemela	soul mate
		amado(a)	loved one
		cariño	darling

"Embrace" these other words!

Girls often receive *descripciones muy especiales*:

¡Qué_____!	How_____!
atractiva	attractive
bella	beautiful
bonita	pretty
hermosa	lovely
linda	very pretty

CHOOSE 'n' USE!

Ese chico es tan . . .	That boy is so . . . (cute, romantic, etc.).
Sí, pero es muy . . . también.	Yes, but he's very . . . (shy, cruel, etc.) too.
Mi . . ., te quiero muchísimo.	My . . . (darling, love, etc.), I love you so much!
Nos conocimos en . . .	We met at a . . . (wedding, concert, etc.).

La religión, la política y la filosofía

You can guess what *la religión*, *la política*, and *la filosofía* mean. And although it's better to avoid such controversial topics in any language, there's a chance they may pop up in a beginning *conversación*. So if you're interested in the *discusión inevitable*, arm yourself with these fiery fundamentals:

Vamos a hablar sobre____.   Let's talk about____.

el Congreso	Congress	*la justicia*	justice
el crimen	crime	*la ley*	law
el espectáculo	entertainment	*la libertad*	freedom
el gobierno	the government	*la moda*	fashion
el medio ambiente	the environment	*la muerte*	death
el presidente	the president	*la paz*	peace
el tráfico	traffic	*la religión*	religion
la ciencia	science	*la sociedad*	society
la Constitución	the Constitution	*la tecnología*	technology
la cultura	culture	*la verdad*	truth
la democracia	democracy	*los viajes espaciales*	space travel
los deportes	sports		
los derechos civiles	civil rights	*Según a . . .*	According to the . . .
los desastres naturales	natural disasters	*la investigación*	research *Según la investigación, el español es fácil de aprender.*
la economía	the economy		
la educación	education		
la elección	election		
la energía	energy	*los hechos*	facts
las fuerzas armadas	the military	*la prueba*	proof
		la evidencia	evidence
la historia	history	*las noticias*	news

To make a negative comment, add *no*.

QUICK TIPS

Estoy de acuerdo.
I agree.
No estoy de acuerdo.
I don't agree.
Lo creo. I believe it.
No lo creo.
I don't believe it.

- The word *mentira* is "a lie" and *mentiroso(a)* is a "liar."
- "To discuss" is *conversar*, but "to argue" is *discutir*.
- As for the court system, you'll mostly hear these *palabras:*

el juez	judge
el juicio	trial
el jurado	jury
el pleito	lawsuit
la prisión	prison
el público	public
tribunal	courtroom

¡Vamos a discutir! (Let's argue!)

Here we go . . . these topics usually stir up *mucha emoción*:

¿Qué piensas de____?	What do you think about____?
el aborto	abortion
el abuso	abuse
las armas	guns
la avaricia	greed
el calentamiento global	global warming
el cambio climático	climate change
el cáncer	cancer
el capitalismo	capitalism
los castigos corporales	corporal punishment
las células madre	stem cells
el comunismo	communism
la contaminación	pollution
el derecho a morir	the right to die
el desempleo	unemployment
las drogas	drugs
la elección	the election
el estrés	stress
la eutanasia	euthanasia
la falta de vivienda	homelessness
el fraude	fraud
el genocidio	genocide

los grandes medios	mainstream media
la guerra	war
el hambre en el mundo	world hunger
la huelga	the strike
los impuestos	taxes
la inmigración	immigration
la libertad religiosa	religious freedom
el matrimonio	marriage
los medios de comunicación	social media
los motines	the riots
la pena capital/ la pena de muerte	capital punishment
la preferencia sexual	sexual preference
el socialismo	socialism
la trata de personas	human trafficking
la vacuna	the vaccine
la violencia	violence

QUICK TIPS

Whenever heavier topics are discussed, play it safe with *comentarios* like . . .
¿Qué piensa de . . .?
What do you think of . . .?
En mi opinión, . . .
In my opinion, . . .
Para mí . . .
To me . . .

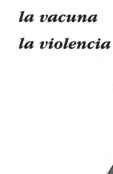

Can you guess what these are about?

la cuarentena

la pandemia

la máscara

la protesta

la distancia social

el virus

Yo creo (I Believe)

Yo creo en_____   **I believe in (the)_____**

el alma	soul	*el infierno*	hell
los ángeles	angels	*Jesucristo*	Jesus Christ
el bautismo	baptism	*los mandamientos*	commandments
la Biblia	Bible	*la mezquita*	mosque
la capilla	chapel	*el milagro*	miracle
el cielo	heaven	*la misa*	church service/ mass
el Corán	Koran		
el coro	choir	*la misercordia*	mercy
la creación	creation	*la muerte*	death
la creencia	belief	*la oración*	prayer
la cruz	cross	*el pecado*	sin
el diablo	devil	*el perdón*	forgiveness
Dios	God	*el sacerdote*	priest
el Espíritu Santo	Holy Spirit	*la salvación*	salvation
la eternidad	eternity	*los santos*	saints
la fe	faith	*el templo*	temple
la gracia	grace	*la vida*	life
la iglesia	church	*la Virgen*	the Virgin

Las religiones

Son_____   **They're_____**

los agnósticos	agnostics	*los hinduistas*	Hindus
los ateos	atheists	*los judíos*	Jews
los budistas	Buddhists	*los mormones*	Mormons
los católicos	Catholics	*los musulmanes*	Moslems/Muslims
la Ciencia Cristiana	Christian Science	*los testigos de Jehová*	Jehovah Witness
los cristianos	Christians		

Los ateos no creen en la Biblia. Atheists don't believe in the Bible

Creo que el diablo vive en el infierno. I believe the Devil lives in hell.

Hay perdón por los pecados. There is forgiveness for sins.

La cultura hispánica

Language and culture are inseparable. Therefore, it's imperative that we take time to look closely at the people who speak Spanish. Who are they? Where do they come from? What are their values, traditions, and lifestyles? Only through understanding one's *cultura* can true communication take place. Chatting is fine, but knowing where the speaker is "coming from" makes all the difference. So do a little research. Read up on Puerto Rican customs, Cuban society, or Mexican history, for example. Learn by asking. Find out about family relationships, foods, and traditional holidays. And keep an open mind. Conversations always become more meaningful when there is mutual respect and consideration.

There's no way we can generalize and stereotype Spanish speakers. Folks from Cuba, Puerto Rico, Mexico, or any other Spanish-speaking country are not all alike. Sure, they share the same language, but each nation's heritage, diet, and everyday conversations differ in several ways. First, let's check out a few *diferencias*. These are considered popular *palabras* among folks from Cuba, Puerto Rico, and Mexico:

Notice carefully "how" people talk! Watch their hands, arms, and facial expressions, especially the eyes. Also, listen for changes in their tone of voice!

Cuba

¡No chive!	Don't bother me!
¿Oigo?	Hello? (on phone)
¡Hola, mi socio!	Hi, pal!
¡Concho!	Darn!
¡Oye, chico, no seas patán!	Hey, don't be a jerk!
Zanjamos el asunto.	Let's solve the problem.
Es un arroz con mango.	It's very complicated.
¡Qué pesado me cae él!	I can't stand him!
Acere, ¿qué bolá?	Buddy, what's up?
¡Qué guayaba!	What a lie!
¡Arranca!	Get going!
Tengo tremenda muela.	I talk too much.

Puerto Rico

¡Oye, tocayo!	Hey, buddy!
No más.	Nothing else.
¡Tranca la boca!	Shut up!
Es la medio guayaba de . . .	She is . . . 's wife.
Saltamos el charco.	Let's fly to New York.
¡Ay, bendito!	Dear Lord!
¡Arrancapa'lante!	Let's get going!
¿Me das pon?	Would you give me a ride?
¡Qué chévere!	Awesome!
¡A mí, plin!	I don't give a darn!
¡A faego!	That's really cool!
¡Ni pa!	No way!

México

¿Mande?	How's that?
¡Pásale!	Go ahead!
¿Bueno?	Hello? (on phone)
¡Ay, chihuahua!	Oh, my gosh!
¿Qué traes?	What's new?
¡Vámonos!	Let's go!
¡Dispensa!	Excuse me!
¡Derecho!	Straight ahead!
¡Qué gacho!	How mean!
¡Ándale!	Hurry up!
¡A poco!	Really!
¿Qué onda?	What's up?
¡Aguas!	Watch out!
¿Neta?	Really?
¡No manches!	You're kidding!
¡Qué padre!	Cool!

Unas palabras básicas
(Some Basic Words)

Cubanas

ajustador	bra	*maní*	peanuts
bala	cigarette	*mima y pipa*	mom and dad
baro	money	*pincha*	job
blumers	underwear	*playera*	sleeveless T-shirt
curda	alcohol		
espejuelos	glasses	*servicio*	toilet
gabo	home	*yin*	jeans
gomas	tires	*yuma*	foreigner
guagua	bus		
jama	food		
jimagua	twin		

Puertorriqueñas

batey	front yard	*guineo*	banana
bembé	party	*mano*	brother
birra	beer	*melón*	watermelon
bodega	grocery store	*negrito*	loved one
broki	friend	*nenos*	children
caucho	sofa	*revolú*	messy
chavo	money	*sombrilla*	umbrella
chino	orange	*tapón*	traffic
compai	pal	*temporal*	hurricane
frisa	blanket		

Mejicanas

alberca	swimming pool	*gavacho*	North American
camión	bus	*guajolote*	turkey
carnal	friend	*huaraches*	sandals
chabacano	apricot	*maíz*	corn
chamacos	children	*mariachis*	musicians
chamarra	jacket	*marqueta*	market
chavalo	boy	*metiche*	nosey
chela	beer	*popote*	drinking straw
crudo	drunk	*sarape*	blanket
feria	money	*tecolote*	owl
		vato	guy

And look online for similar regional words and expressions if you plan to travel to other Spanish-speaking countries.

Las comidas tradicionales (Traditional Foods)

Here are a few popular *platos "dishes"* served throughout Mexico, Cuba, and Puerto Rico. I recommend them all!

Comida cubana (Cuban Food)

ajiaco vegetable and meat soup

arroz a la cubana white rice and fried egg

arroz congrí rice with black beans

arroz con leche rice, milk, and sugar

arroz con pollo rice with chicken

boniatos sweet potatoes

chambarete lamb shanks

empanada meat pie

frijoles negros black beans

malanga root vegetable

mojito popular drink

picadillo spicy hash

ropa vieja shredded beef

tostones banana chips

yuca con mojo potato-like vegetable

Comida puertorriqueña (Puerto Rican Food)

adobo meat marinade

arañas shredded plantains

arroz con gándules exotic rice and bean dish

arroz guisado stew and rice

arroz y habichuelas rojas rice and kidney beans

bacalao pickled codfish

camarones al ajillo shrimp in butter sauce

chayote relleno stuffed squash

gandinga pork and kidney stew

mofongo large fried green banana dish

pasteles husk-wrapped dish

quesito cream cheese pastry

sofrito spicy seasoning

vianda starchy vegetables

Ask "how" certain foods are eaten, and of course, "how" they are prepared!

Comida mejicana (Mexican Food)

barbacoa BBQ lamb

birria shredded goat meat

bolillos rolls

buñuelos deep fried donuts

burrito wrapped and filled flour tortilla

carne asada grilled beef strips

carnitas roast pork

chile relleno stuffed pepper

churros sugary cinnamon roll sticks

enchiladas soft-wrapped corn tortilla, usually with cheese

flan vanilla pudding

flautas deep-fried taco

frijoles refried beans, of course

guacamole avocado sauce

huevos rancheros eggs with salsa

lengua cow's tongue

menudo tripe soup

mole chicken, turkey, or pork in sauce

nopales diced cactus

pan dulce Mexican pastry

pozole soup with pork

quesadilla cheese on tortillas

sope small, pizza-like tortilla

taco soft, not hard

tamal wrapped in corn husk

tortillas round, flat wheat or corn meal wrap heated on a grill

tostada flat and fried tortilla

¿PUEDE RECORDARLO?
(Can You Remember It?)

☑ Name five words that tell "when?"

☑ Name five words that tell "where?"

☑ Name five words that relate to sports.

☑ Name three toys.

☑ Name five words you may need on a trip.

☑ Name three words that relate to love.

☑ Name five words that relate to religion, politics, or philosophy.

☑ What's your favorite Mexican, Cuban, or Puerto Rican food?

10

CHAPTER *DIEZ*

Las últimas palabras

(Last Words)

Talk about Language

Eventually, during the Spanish learning experience you will be forced to communicate with the "language" words commonly found in textbooks. Do you remember these from English class?

el adjetivo	adjective	*"Grande" es un adjetivo.*
el adverbio	adverb	*La palabra "rápidamente" es un adverbio.*
el capítulo	chapter	*Me gusta el capítulo diez.*
la conjugación	conjugation	*No entiendo la conjugación de los verbos.*

la consonante	consonant	*la pregunta*	question
el diálogo	dialogue	*el pronombre*	pronoun
la escritura	writing	*la pronunciación*	pronunciation
la estructura	structure	*la puntuación*	punctuation
el ejemplo	example	*el repaso*	review
el ejercicio	exercise	*el significado*	meaning
el estudio	study	*el sonido*	sound
el examen	test	*el sujeto*	subject
la frase	sentence	*el sustantivo*	noun
la gramática	grammar	*la tarea*	homework
el habla	speech	*el tema*	theme
el idioma	language	*el tiempo verbal*	tense
la lección	lesson	*la traducción*	translation
la lectura	reading	*el verbo*	verb
la mayúscula	capital letter	*el vocabulario*	vocabulary
la minúscula	lower case letter	*la vocal*	vowel
la página	page	*la voz*	voice
la palabra	word		

 "Language" is also called *el lenguaje* or *la lengua*.

Other things you might say:

El estudio de la gramática no es muy importante.
The study of grammar is not very important.
¡Comprendo el significado del vocabulario!
I understand the meaning of the vocabulary!
Necesito más ejercicios y repaso.
I need more exercises and review.
¡No hay exámenes ni tareas!
There are no tests or homework!

La computadora (The Computer)

Chances are your computer, smartphone, or other digital device will play a major part in your language learning experience. Not only is the Internet packed with free Spanish learning websites, but the number of free Spanish learning apps is on the rise! In Spanish, computer vocabulary is often spelled the same as in English (***el e-mail, la wifi, el laptop, las apps, el streaming, etc***.). However, these other words might be useful, too:

Voy a . . .	**I'm going . . .**
apagar	to shut down
archivar	to file
arrastrar	to drag
buscar	to search
cargar	to upload
compartir	to share
conectar	to connect
cortar y pegar	to cut and paste
descargar	to download
editar	to edit
eliminar	to delete
encontrar	to find
enviar	to send
escoger	to select
googlear	to Google search
guardar	to save
hacer clic/cliquear	to click
hacer copia	to copy
importar	to import
imprimir	to print

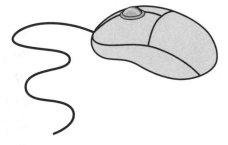

instalar	to install
prender	to boot up
recibir	to receive
reenviar	to forward
responder	to reply
sincronizar	to sync

¿Dónde está . . .?	**Where's the . . .?**
la dirección	address (email)
el adjunto	attachment
la copia de seguridad	back-up
el favorito	bookmark
el navegador	browser
el botón	button
el cable	cable
la cargadora	charger
el código	code
el cursor	cursor
los datos	data
los audífonos	ear buds
el correo electrónico	email
el archivo	file
la carpeta	folder
la página inicial	home page
el icono	icon
el teclado	keyboard
la portátil	laptop
el enlace	link
el buzón	mailbox
la memoria	memory
el menú	menu
el mensaje	message
el ratón	mouse
la red	network
la contraseña	password

la plataforma	platform
el enchufe	plug
el puerto	port
la impresora	printer
la pantalla	screen
el buscador	search engine
el servidor	server
la pestaña	tab (in a browser)
la barra de herramientas	tool bar
la basura	trash
el nombre de usario	user name
el video	video
la página web	web page
el sitio web	web site
la ventana	window

¡Hable inglés!

You're in luck! Countless tech words stay in English, often using the business or program's title or name. These are some examples:

Me gusta . . . I like . . .

iCloud, Zoom, Instagram, Facebook, Twitter, Microsoft, Apple, iPad, Word, Excel, Google, Yahoo, Safari, Firefox, Snapchat, WhatsApp, YouTube, Spotify, Reddit, Bitcoin, Netflix, Ring, iPhone, Amazon, etc.

The same goes for many words related to your life in this techno-age. Just speak English!

app, chat, internet, hashtag, selfie, memes, streaming, text, spam, emoticon, Facetime, podcast, blog, GIF, PDF, JPEG, QR, etc.

Some words you'll have to look up, especially those referring to the latest trends in technology.

artificial intelligence	*inteligencia artificial*
internet of things	*internet de los objetos*
self-driving cars	*coches/carros/autos sin conductor*

QUICK TIPS

- *Es inalámbrico.* (It's wireless.)
- Here are the parts of an email:
  Juan *nombre del usario*
  user name

  @ *arroba*
  at

  Spanish Provider *el nombre del dominio/ el proveedor del acceso* domain name/ access provider

  . punto
  dot

  pe *país*
  country

 Notice that *.com, .edu, .org,* etc. are not normal closings to an e-mail in other countries. In many cases, the country such as *.fr* (France), *.es* (Spain), and *.pe* (Peru) each have their own abbreviation. BTW "slash" (/) is *la barra* and "backslash" (\) is *la barra invertida.*

Práctica, práctica, práctica

Traditionally, foreign language "practice" involved completion of grammar exercises, dialogue memorization, and hours of audio-lingual drills in a language lab. Good news! Practice techniques have changed – and, in my opinion, – for the better. The following methods are currently being applied to many areas of learning worldwide in the most successful programs.

Learning Basic *Pronunciación*

If Spanish is not your first language, it'll take time to improve your pronunciation. Your brain (and mouth) are already locked into the language you normally speak. The only way you'll get better is by practicing. These techniques will help.

Trabalenguas (Tongue Twisters)

Even though going online, listening to and then repeating words will help, for real language fun, why not try this other effective practice technique. They're called tongue-twisters! This exercise will not only help your pronunciation skills, but you can also acquire new Spanish words. How fast can you say these one-liners without hurting yourself?

Tres tristes tigres trillaron trigo en un trigal.
Three sad tigers threshed wheat in a wheat field.

Compre poca capa parda, porque el que poca capa parda compra poca capa parda paga.
Buy only a little brown cape, for he who buys only a little brown cape pays only for a little brown cape.

Pepe Pecas pica papas con un pico, con un pico pica papas Pepe Pecas.
Joe Freckles chops potatoes with a pick, with a pick Joe Freckles chops potatoes.

Otra vez, por favor (Again, Please)

Don't deny it. Sometimes you get lost when someone is speaking Spanish to you. You stammer away and then get confused about how to pronounce your words correctly. Well, just try to relax and do the best you can with the phrases below. You'll be glad you did!

More slowly, please.	*Más despacio, por favor.*
I'm sorry.	*Lo siento.*
I'm trying the best I can.	*Estoy intentando lo mejor que puedo.*
I don't pronounce well.	*No pronuncio bien.*
I speak a little Spanish.	*Hablo poquito español.*
I'm learning Spanish.	*Estoy aprendiendo español.*
I don't remember the word.	*No recuerdo la palabra.*
I don't know.	*No sé.*
I don't understand.	*No entiendo.*
Thanks for your patience.	*Gracias por su paciencia.*
Can you repeat that?	*¿Puede repetirlo?*
What does it mean?	*¿Qué significa?*
Do you understand?	*¿Entiende usted?*
How do you say it?	*¿Cómo se dice?*

La guía (The Guide)

Keep a photo of this pronunciation guide on your phone. It can help whenever you forget how to say a Spanish word correctly – with or without an accent mark.

Guide to Spanish Sound-making

* Spanish words are pronounced exactly the way they are written.

* Knowing the **BIG 5** (vowels) is the key to speaking and understanding Spanish.

* Poor pronunciation in Spanish does not seriously affect communication, so do the best you can.

- Turn up the volume for the accented (´) parts of words. Spanish words without accents get more volume at the end, unless they end in *A, E, I, O, U, N,* or *S.* These get more volume on the next to the last part.

- Spanish words are "run-together" in short, choppy pieces, usually pronounced in the front part of the mouth, with little or no air being used to make the sounds.

Learning Basic *Vocabulario*

Without vocabulary, you'll end up repeating the same "baby words" over and over again. Here are some ways to help build up your *vocabulario*:

- Before anything else, download a free vocabulary "flashcard app." Not only can you create your own vocabulary flashcards, but some apps include games and exercises for vocabulary review and practice.

- Use the command words! Combine them with names of things you'd like to know. Use real objects or pictures of items. Have a friend "order you" to touch or move whatever it is you're learning. *¡Toque este libro!* (Touch this book!)

- Interview Spanish speakers. List items like sports or foods and ask individuals which ones they like or dislike. Use a question, *¿Le gusta a Ud. . . .?* "Do you like . . .?" and check off their responses.

- Collect Spanish children's books, coloring books, or interactive toys. Since you're a "child" in the Spanish language, it's important to have lots of visual exposure to new words. While reading, point to each picture and "name it" in *español*. (This is really fun to do with the kids!)

- Make an audio (or video) recording. Ask a native Spanish speaker to read aloud a list of words that you need to know. Record different people, so you can hear all the different sounds. At first, don't bother with vocabulary you're not going to use every day. And offer to make an English recording in return!

¡Dibújelo! (Draw It!)

Draw pictures of items in special categories, and then label them. The more "unartistic" learners can find free pictures or clipart on the internet!

Las comidas (Foods)

| *manzana* | *plátano* | *cereza* | *coco* | *melón* |

Although it's not always feasible, these activities work better when learners are assisted by native Spanish-speakers. And be creative! For example, practice descriptive words by downloading photos of either a strange-looking monster or your celebrity dream date.

If you've got the time, cut out pictures of objects from a magazine and make games like Bingo or Concentration. (Great way to spend time with the family!)

muy gorda
cuatro brazos
tres ojos
orejas grandes

mucho dinero
pelo largo
muy bonita
superinteligente

¡Cante una canción! (Sing a Song!)

Get somebody who knows something about music to play or sing traditional Spanish serenades for you. Memorize them, and you'll fit right in at any Hispanic social event! Start off with the classic example below. As you practice, jot down all the new vocabulary.

Las mañanitas	
Estas son las mañanitas	These are the little songs
que cantaba el rey David	that King David would sing
a las muchachas bonitas,	to the pretty girls,
se las cantaban así:	he'd sing to them like this:
Despierta, mi bien, despierta.	Wake up, my love, wake up.
Mira, que ya amaneció.	Look, the dawn has come.
Ya los pajaritos cantan.	The birds are already singing.
La luna ya se metió.	The moon is down.

¡Baile al ritmo! (Dance to the Rhythm!)

Dancing is yet another excellent approach to learning new vocabulary. It's true! Take a class in Latin dance and you'll be chattering away in no time. The *cha-cha*, *cumbia*, *salsa*, *samba*, *mambo*, and *merengue* are the most popular steps, and Latin tunes are available everywhere. By listening to the chorus time and again, the words will stick, and your Spanish will improve. More importantly, you'll be having fun, and be able to join in at Latino parties or clubs. Who knows? Maybe your fancy steps will lead you to exciting new relationships!

Song and dance can be tremendous language experiences, but don't stop there. Here's a list of other "extra-curricular" activities that are filled with Hispanic cultural environment. Consult your local news media about upcoming events involving folks from Spain or Latin America.

holiday celebrations	sports competitions	operas	ballets
plays	movies	cooking classes	concerts
shows	museum displays	conferences	family parties
festivals	workshops	seminars	blogs and podcasts

Add more ideas if you're in the mood!

_____

_____

_____

Learning Basic *Conversación*

The best advice I can offer to those wanting experience in basic Spanish conversation is to **just do it**! However, to practice "chit-chatting" on your own, here are two helpful suggestions.

BillTalks

¡Yo hablo español! Check the app for more on conversations.

Los dibujos animados (Cartoons)

One fun way is to play with any drawing program or app, first by creating a few cartoon characters, and then by making up a few "foreign" responses that relate to the pictures. Stick with Spanish words you already know. Here's a sample cartoon with the words "whited-out." Just write in or even audio record something that fits.

Bien, gracias. ¿Y usted?

Muchas gracias. Adiós.

Los diálogos (Dialogues)

On a document, create a *diálogo* of your own and then print it out. Be sure it's one that you really need and will use often. With scissors, cut out each sentence or phrase. Then, mix them up. Now, try putting the pieces back in order so that the dialogue makes sense.

Bien. ¿Dónde está José?

De nada. Hasta luego.

Hablando por teléfono (Talking on the Phone)

How are your phone skills in Spanish? Now there's a real conversation challenge! Next time you misdial and a Spanish speaker answers, don't hang up! Listen very carefully, and practice these expressions:

José está en la oficina.

Hello!	*¡Aló!* or *¡Diga!* or *¡Bueno!*
This is _____.	*Este es _____.*
Please don't hang up.	*No cuelgue, por favor.*
Please wait a moment.	*Espere un momento, por favor.*
Could I speak with ___?	*¿Puedo hablar con _____?*
Is he/she at home?	*¿Está en casa?*
When will he/she return?	*¿Cuándo regresa?*
May I leave a message?	*¿Puedo dejar un mensaje?*
Could I take a message?	*¿Puedo tomar un mensaje?*
I'll call back later.	*Llamaré más tarde.*

Hola. ¿Cómo está?

| Please, call me at ____. | *Por favor, llámeme al número _____.* |
| Is there someone there who speaks English? | *¿Hay alguien allí que hable inglés?* |

Los proverbios (Proverbs)

Proverbs are meaningful words to the wise, and they are exchanged in Spanish conversations everyday. Check out the following gems, and memorize those that suit you best. Can you create an English equivalent?

Al que madruga, Dios lo ayuda.
He who gets up early, God helps.   =   The early bird catches the worm.

Dime con quién andas, y te diré quién eres.
Tell me who you hang around with, and I'll tell you who you are.

En boca cerrada no entran moscas.
Flies do not enter a closed mouth.

No todo lo que brilla es oro.
All that glitters is not gold.

Más vale pájaro en mano que ciento volando.
A bird in hand is worth one hundred flying.

No dejes para mañana lo que puedes hacer hoy.
Don't leave for tomorrow what you can do today.

Camarón que se duerme se lo lleva la corriente.
The shrimp that sleeps, the current takes away.

Donde una puerta se cierra, otra se abre.
Whenever a door closes, another opens.

Donde no hay amor, no hay dolor.
Where there is no love, there is no pain.

Learning Basic *Acciones*

Unquestionably, the most natural way to acquire verbs or "action words" is by having someone command you "to do something," In acting out the command, you "pick up" on the action word used. Here's another suggestion. With "visuals," you can begin to "talk" about what's going on, and creating your own "visuals" is easy! All you need are some paper, a printer, and access to free photos or clip art on the internet. Use the model given below, or develop your own. Get friends and family to join you. Let that imagination run wild! Here's a "visual" chart that helps teach the affirmative, negative, and question forms. Try these with the action word ***comiendo*** (eating).

With a chart, we can expand on the action words. Be sure you begin with a column of people who represent the subject pronouns (**I, You, He, She, They,** and **We**). The visuals can be "read," as you can see with the answers below.

> Continue searching for a fun (and free) Spanish language video game to play on your smart phone! Find one with good graphics and simple situations. Listen for any vocabulary and verbs you've learned so far.

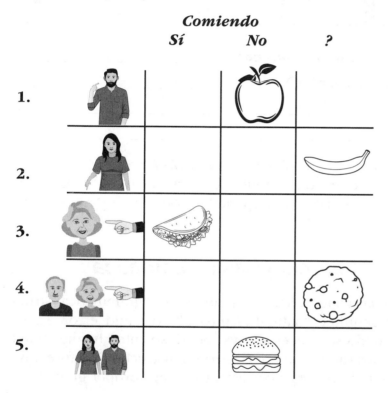

Comiendo

Sí   *No*   *?*

1.
2.
3.
4.
5.

1. *No, yo no estoy comiendo manzanas.*

2. _____ .

3. *Sí, ella está comiendo tacos.*

4. *¿Ustedes están comiendo naranjas?*

5. *No, nosotros* _____ .

El Storyboard

A storyboard is for the superstar who already knows a bunch of action words. Go box to box, and tell "what's happening in each picture now." Only use the "present progressive" tense.

El hombre está durmiendo. _____

The man is sleeping. _____

_____   _____

_____   _____

When you get really ***bueno en español***, you'll also be able to answer questions about the story, such as "What happened?" or "What has happened?". You're really not that far away!

Learning Basic *Gramática*

As in all languages, Spanish grammar or "grammatical structure" is acquired "naturally" through trial and error. That's why a child's sentences always sound "so cute." It takes years of mistakes (and hours of classroom instruction) before anyone is able to respond consistently using "proper grammar."

Fortunately, for second-language learners there is a shortcut. Scientific studies indicate that reading is one way to "fast and painless" language acquisition. Thus, by reading Spanish, learners can "pick up" basic rules of ***la gramática española***. It seems that when the rest of us read simple, interesting stories regularly, our spoken Spanish improves, and our grammar usage becomes ***correcto*** most of the time!

The following is a brief story filled with grammar information introduced in Chapters 3 to 8. Before you read it, go back and skim the chapters. Then, read through the story. Next, check the chapters again to confirm your comprehension.

Children's books work very well for adults learning beginning Spanish grammar!

BillTalks

83

¡Yo hablo español! Check the app for a short story to test how much you've learned.

Lea una historia (Read a Story)

Yo soy <u>Roberto</u>. Ahora estoy muy <u>bien</u>. Tengo <u>28</u> años y no tengo muchos <u>problemas</u>. Estoy trabajando para una compañía <u>grande</u> en <u>los Estados Unidos</u> con muchos de mis amigos. Me gusta mi trabajo. Me gusta mi familia, también. Todos son de <u>México</u>. En mi casa están mi <u>esposa</u>, <u>mis hijos</u>, mi <u>madre</u> y mi <u>abuelo</u>. La casa es <u>grande</u>. Tiene <u>cuatro</u> dormitorios, <u>tres</u> baños, una cocina <u>grande</u> y la sala. Pero no hay <u>garaje</u>. Es un problema porque tengo un carro <u>nuevo</u>. Es un <u>Toyota</u> blanco.

Mi <u>esposa</u> y mi <u>madre</u> están trabajando ahora en <u>un restaurante</u>. Están muy <u>contentas</u> allí. <u>Mis hijos</u> están estudiando en <u>las escuelas públicas</u>. Son muy <u>inteligentes</u>. Están estudiando <u>inglés</u>. Mi <u>abuelo</u> no está trabajando porque tiene problemas con la <u>espalda</u>.

El <u>lunes</u> no voy a trabajar. Estoy preparando todo para un viaje a <u>México</u>. Cada <u>diciembre</u> toda la familia tiene una fiesta grande en nuestro <u>pueblo</u>. El <u>pueblo</u> está en las <u>montañas</u> y es necesario comprar mucha <u>comida</u> y <u>ropa</u> especial. Por ahora, estoy trabajando horas extra para pagar el viaje.

Ahora estoy trabajando "overtime".

When you do Spanish readings like this, remember that "open-ended" techniques are used in stories to teach both grammar and vocabulary. Certain words are deleted, and readers insert any appropriate (or funny) vocabulary. So "exchange" the underlined words for others! The same could be done with the action words! Personal tales involving daily activities appear to work best.

QUICK TIPS

- Find out how to switch your device from English to Spanish text! You will understand very little at first, but perseverance and imagination will get you far.
- Collect varied Spanish reading materials! In addition to books, e-books, and magazines, gather inserts, labels, brochures, flyers, forms, and even posters. Remember words with pictures are always ideal.
- *Librerías* (bookstores), *bibliotecas* (libraries), *papelerías* (stationery stores), and *quioscos* (newsstands) sell or loan out literature for all reading levels. Many are found online. (Browsing in these places is nice, because you don't have to say a word!)
- Avoid stopping to "study" words and sentences! Calmly skim over what you don't understand and try to focus on the main idea of each paragraph.
- At home, practice reading aloud. Record yourself, play it back, and then note any obvious "sound-making" problems. Maybe you can "read along" with native Spanish speakers!
- Download a Spanish learning app on your smartphone or tablet today!

Unas preguntas (Some Questions)

Grammar improves the more we correct ourselves. Here are 22 "grammar-packed" ***preguntas*** you should now be able to answer. Keep trying until you get it right . . . and ***por favor***, be brief!

¿Cómo está usted?

¿Cómo se llama usted?

¿Cuál es su número de teléfono?

¿Quién es su doctor?

¿De quién es este libro?

¿Le gusta a usted la música clásica?

¿Qué hora es?

¿Qué día es hoy?

¿Qué tiempo hace?

¿Cuáles son tres partes del cuerpo?

¿Cuántas hermanas tiene usted?

¿Hay un perro en su casa?

¿Dónde trabaja usted?

¿Es muy bonita la Mona Lisa?

¿Dónde está su cama?

¿Es usted de los Estados Unidos?

¿Tiene usted hambre?

¿Cuántos años tiene usted?

¿Qué está haciendo usted?

¿Qué están haciendo los miembros de su familia?

¿Cuándo habla usted español?

¿Qué hay detrás de usted?

Feeling brave? Try these!

¿Sabe usted mucho español?

¿Adónde va usted mañana?

¿Se lava usted las manos todos los días?

¿Quién fue el primer presidente de los Estados Unidos?

¿Dónde estaba usted anoche?

¿Quiere usted ir a Disneylandia?

¿Tiene usted miedo de los gatos negros?

¿Puede usted jugar al fútbol?

¿De dónde es usted?

¿Qué hace si ve el letrero "empuje"?

The Answers to these Questions? Just write 'em or just say 'em! And then, you'll have to check 'em yourself!

Before I Say *Adiós* . . .

Without a doubt, this was the most difficult part of the entire guidebook to write. What more can I say? Everything you really need to get started in Spanish has already been introduced. (I know, because I once was in your *zapatos*.) Nevertheless, to make it all really work, I decided to summarize my thoughts in a series of closing remarks, personal comments and easy-to-follow suggestions which, when considered, lead "the rest of us" to immediate success in Spanish. *Por favor*, take heed.

The Giant Steps to *Comunicación*

SEE HOW YOU HAVE "CLIMBED" FROM *MUY POQUITO* TO *MUCHO ESPAÑOL*!

Fourth: Advanced Spanish . . . and beyond!

(mucho más vocabulario y gramática)
Third: You need to use the *"-ndo's"* and other action word forms.

(más vocabulario y gramática)
Second: You've got to feel comfortable about using *ser* and *estar* (and even *tener*).

(vocabulario y gramática)
First: You have to know the "Secrets to Sound-making" and basic survival words.

Cosas to Always Keep in Mind

- Pronunciation and grammar don't matter that much!
- You don't have to speak until you feel like doing it!
- Feeling comfortable around non-English speakers makes a difference!
- You can't make any excuses for not learning!
- Language learning takes place when you relax and have fun!

The *Secretos* to Success

(All of these have already been mentioned. They are all *muy, muy importantes!*)

- Try to be sensitive to and aware of cultural differences.
- Get in the habit of using Spanish regularly.
- Constantly memorize vocabulary through "word-picture" association.
- Experiment, take chances, and guess when you are unsure!
- Follow the practice tips and activities mentioned throughout **Spanish for the Rest of Us**.
- Add your own ideas on how to practice and improve! This guidebook only establishes a base for your entire Spanish learning experience. Ask around, listen, and "build" from here.

 Do not memorize these rules! Simply be aware of the problems facing the beginner! And as always, remember that "being close" is good enough. Besides, all of this stuff is picked up *muy rápido* once you actually get started.

- Memorizing jokes, tongue-twisters, rhymes, and songs is a fantastic way to gain confidence while learning language skills.
- Spanish speakers of different countries don't all agree! It's not uncommon for them to "clash" over meanings of words, customs, or historical events. That's why it's important to be aware of the differences between Hispanic dialects. Try to be good at guessing where folks are from!

Some *Más* Advice

- Try relaxation techniques before you "go for it." Stress-relief information is available everywhere.

- Don't "stop in the middle" to translate! Whenever you're listening, concentrate on the topic first, so that you have some idea of what's going on.

- Aggressive, outgoing, fun-loving people (like the rest of us) usually learn Spanish faster than others. A childlike attitude also seems to help!

- When you are in an embarrassing situation, stuck, confused, or at a loss for Spanish words, rely on these for help: *Lo siento.* (I'm sorry.) *No recuerdo la palabra.* (I don't remember the word.) *Estoy estudiando español.* (I'm studying Spanish.)

- Again, please say *por favor*. In Spanish, you'll go far if you are courteous. The more respectful you are, the more Spanish you'll learn. So practice "polite" things to say. And as always, be sincere.

- Try to be patient! I know what the word "busy" means – but life's too short to pass up those rare opportunities to practice talking Spanish with someone. Trust me, take the extra moments now or later you'll regret not doing so.

- Some words mean two or more things in Spanish. Find out the appropriate use for each meaning. Online translators or dictionaries often help, but be careful! (It's always better to go straight to the source.)

Problemas the Rest of Us Seem to Have

- The **Secrets to Sound-making**

  Even though pronunciation doesn't need to be practiced, becoming familiar with the "Big Five and the Others" will definitely make understanding and speaking a whole lot easier. (In particular, watch out for the *e*, *a*, and *i*!) Remember, in Spanish you always pronounce the letters the same. There are no exceptions!

- The *El* and *La* **Business**

  Again, although it won't affect communication much, practice putting *la* in front of objects ending with *a*, and *el* before those ending with *o*. (You'll just have to remember which one goes with words not ending in *o* or *a*.)

- **The Reversal Rule**

  When describing things, giving the date, or telling "whose," think backward! In these instances, the Spanish word order is "reversed".

- **The Once-and-for-All Rule**

  Another pattern that should be mentioned is the way in which strings of words have to "agree" in Spanish. "Agreement" is best understood by observing some examples. Notice how the words "agree" with each other:

Los libros buenos	The good books
La muchacha bonita	The pretty girl
Muchas casas negras y blancas	Lots of black and white houses

- **Confusing words**

  Here are a handful of *palabras* that always seem to bother the rest of us. Pay close attention – they're "sneaky":

poquito	a little bit	*número*	number
pequeño	small in size	*nombre*	name
de nada	you're welcome	*qué*	what
nada	nothing	*que*	that
muy	very	*dólar*	dollar
mucho	a lot	*dolor*	pain

sí	yes	*hombre*	man
si	if	*hambre*	hunger
grande	large	*nuevo*	new
largo	long	*nueve*	nine
bueno	good		
bien	fine		

- *Por vs. para*
  Students of Spanish have been struggling with these two forever. They both mean "for," but are used differently. Maybe these examples will help:

The word *por* expresses:

Motion/place: *El perro corre por la casa.* (The dog runs through the house.)

Means/manner: *Llega por Amazon.* (It arrives by Amazon.)

In exchange for/substitution: *Voy a hacerlo por ti.* (I'm going to do it for you.)

Duration of an action: *He vivido en Cuba por ocho años.* (I've lived in Cuba for eight years.)

Indefinite time period: *Descanso por la tarde.* (I rest in the afternoon.)

On behalf of: *Estoy trabajando por Ud.* (I am working on your behalf.)

Per: *Cuesta un dólar por taco.* (It costs a dollar per taco.)

These sentences will help you remember when to use *por* and when to use *para*!

The word *para* expresses:

Destination/place: ***Salimos para Nueva York.*** (We are leaving for New York.)

Destination/person: ***El dinero es para Ud.*** (The money is for you.)

A future time limit: ***Es para mañana.*** (It's for tomorrow.)

Purpose/goal: ***Bailo para divertirme.*** (I dance to have fun.)

Use/function: ***Es un cepillo para los dientes.*** (It's a tooth-brush.)

Comparisons: ***Para su edad, lee bien.*** (For her age, she reads well.)

Opinion: ***Para mí, está demasiado crudo.*** (For me it's too rare.)

"TEN TALKING TIPS"
FOR THE REST OF US

1   Confusing the vowel sounds, such as hearing the "*i*" and thinking it's an "*e*."

2   Confusing certain consonant sounds, such as hearing the "*j*" sound and thinking it's an "*h*."

3   Pronouncing words with "*rr*" without rolling the "*r*'s," such as saying "*caro*" (expensive) instead of "*carro*" (car).

4   Pronouncing words with "*ll*" as if it were "*l*," such as saying *"polo"* (shirt) instead of *"pollo"* (chicken).

5   Pronouncing words with "*ñ*" as if they were "*n*," such as saying "*cana*" (gray hair) instead of "*caña*" (sugarcane).

6   Mispronouncing words due to not understanding accentuation, such as saying "*esta*" (this) instead of "*está*" (is).

7   Pronouncing the "*gue*" and "*gui*" in Spanish like "gway" and "gwee."

8   Pronouncing the "*que*" and "*qui*" in Spanish like "kway" and "kwee."

9   Forgetting that the "*z*" is pronounced as an "*s*" in Spanish.

10   Forgetting that the "*v*" is pronounced more like a "*b*" in Spanish.

"TEN GRAMMAR TIPS" FOR THE REST OF US

1 Translating literally, such as saying "*Estoy frío*" instead of "*Tengo frío*" to express "I'm cold."

2 Getting the gender of nouns mixed up, such as incorrectly saying, "*la problema*" instead of "*el problema*."

3 Forgetting to reverse the order of adjectives and nouns in a sentence, such as saying, "*grande casa*" instead of "*casa grande*."

4 Forgetting that "*la gente*" (people) is singular in Spanish, such as saying, "*La gente están aquí.*" instead of "*La gente está aquí.*" It's different in English, where we say, "The people are here."

5 Not distinguishing between the informal "*tú*" and the formal "*usted*" forms, such as addressing a stranger with "*¿Cómo estás tú?*" instead of "*¿Cómo está usted?*" to ask "How are you?"

6 Forgetting to apply a double negative, such as saying "*Hay nadie*" instead of "*No hay nadie*" to express "There is no one."

7 Guessing incorrectly at cognate word translations, such as hearing "*sopa*" (soup) and thinking it means "soap".

8 Overusing the subject pronouns, such as constantly adding "*yo*" (I) before verbs in a sentence even when it's already understood who's doing the talking.

9 Mixing up the verbs *ser* and *estar*, such as saying "*Estoy estudiante*" instead of "*Soy estudiante*" to express "I am a student."

10 Applying regular verb conjugations upon irregular verbs, such as saying "*sabo*" instead of "*sé*" to express "I know."

Add some more problem areas of your own!

¿PUEDE RECORDARLO?
(Can You Remember It?)

☑ Name five Spanish words that are found in a typical grammar book.

☑ Name five Spanish words that refer to working on a computer.

☑ Give one tip that will help you improve your pronunciation skills in Spanish.

☑ Give one tip that will help you improve your vocabulary skills in Spanish.

☑ Give one tip that will help you improve your conversation skills in Spanish.

☑ Give one tip that will help you improve your use of verbs or "action words" in Spanish.

☑ Give one tip that will help you improve your grammar skills in Spanish.

☑ Name three common problems the rest of us struggle with in learning Spanish.

Últimas palabras (Final Words)

It's entirely up to you how much *español* you'll eventually speak and understand. I hope that the easy-to-follow format has made your learning experience enjoyable – free of the stress and frustration of traditional programs. And probably by now you've discovered how the guidebook can be used to get best results. Use **Spanish for the Rest of Us** any way you'd like! Set your own pace, take what you need, and reread only those pages that interest you. Some degree of language acquisition is guaranteed.

But this is really only the beginning. At the moment, you're merely crawling, standing, or staggering in the language. Trust me, fellow *estudiantes*, the best is yet to come.

Hasta luego, amigos,
Bill and Cecilia

BillTalks
84

¡Yo hablo español! Check the app for more suggestions and reminders to help improve your Spanish.

Personal Success Chart

Date	Mi experiencia
2 de marzo	I used a greeting!
18 de abril	I understood my Spanish-speaking neighbor!

_____

_____

_____

_____

_____

_____

_____

_____

_____

_____

_____

Translation Review!

Connect each word with its correct translation:

Colors	Los colores	The class	La clase
black	morado	book	pluma
green	rojo	pencil	papel
white	verde	paper	libro
purple	negro	table	lápiz
red	blanco	pen	mesa

Expressions	Las expresiones		
Good idea	Quizás	It's true	Yo tampoco
Me, too	Creo que sí	I'm so glad	Con razón
Maybe	Sin duda	No doubt	Me alegro
I think so	Yo también	Me, neither	Es verdad
No wonder	Buena idea	That's OK	Está bien

Questions	Las preguntas
What?	¿Dónde?
How much?	¿Quién?
Where?	¿Qué?
Who?	¿Cuál?
Which?	¿Cuánto?

Pronouns	Los pronombres
She	Ellos
He	Ustedes
We	Él
They	Ella
You guys	Nosotros

Numbers	Los números
10	doce
18	treinta
12	diez
15	dieciocho
30	quince

Connect each word with its correct translation.

Days of the week	Los días de la semana
Monday	miércoles
Saturday	domingo
Sunday	lunes
Thursday	sábado
Wednesday	jueves

The weather	El clima
clear	lluvia
sun	frío
cold	despejado
snow	nieve
rain	sol

Feelings	Los sentimientos
well	ocupado
busy	preocupado
surprised	bien
angry	sorprendido
worried	enojado

Body parts	Las partes del cuerpo
back	estómago
throat	espalda
stomach	dedo
head	pierna
tooth	cabeza
leg	rodilla
eye	cuello
finger	garganta
neck	ojo
knee	diente

Connect each word with its correct translation.

The family	La familia
father	hijo
sister	esposa
grandfather	tío
daughter	hermana
mother	marido
aunt	abuelo
uncle	hija
wife	tía
husband	madre
son	padre

Occupations	Las ocupaciones
chef	bombero
surgeon	cajero
student	granjero
gardener	cirujano
cashier	jardinero
teacher	estudiante
plumber	camarero
waiter	profesor
farmer	plomero
firefighter	cocinero

Work	El trabajo
contract	copiadora
mail	almacén
strike	fábrica
product	horario
tool	huelga
copier	correo
factory	herramienta
schedule	contrato
warehouse	producto

Connect each word with its correct translation.

Descriptions	*Las descripciones*
bad	*equivocado*
old	*guapo*
good	*viejo*
tall	*malo*
handsome	*blando*
inexpensive	*rubio*
empty	*vacío*
soft	*bueno*
wrong	*barato*
blond	*alto*

The house	*La casa*
closet	*escoba*
dryer	*trapeador*
rug	*espejo*
curtains	*cortinas*
mop	*alfombra*
washer	*plancha*
broom	*lavadora*
mirror	*sábanas*
iron	*secadora*
sheets	*ropero*

Rooms	*Los cuartos*
bedroom	*sala*
basement	*cocina*
kitchen	*dormitorio*
living room	*baño*
bathroom	*sótano*

Connect each word with its correct translation.

Tools	Las herramientas
screwdriver	escalera
hose	rastrillo
saw	destornillador
rake	manguera
ladder	serrucho

The city	La ciudad
library	supermercado
post office	escuela
shoe store	biblioteca
church	gasolinera
supermarket	zapatería
pharmacy	tienda
bakery	oficina de correo
store	farmacia
gas station	panadería
school	iglesia

Transportation	El transporte
train	avión
boat	autobús
bicycle	tren
bus	bote
airplane	bicicleta

Animals	Los animales
duck	caballo
bird	gato
dog	pájaro
horse	perro
cat	pato
sheep	vaca
mouse	puerco
cow	oveja
pig	ratón

Connect each word with its correct translation.

Food	La comida
steak	pollo
cookie	helado
bread	galleta
ice cream	bistec
turkey	pastel
lobster	pan
cake	pavo
candy	langosta
butter	dulce
chicken	mantequilla

Drinks	Las bebidas
milkshake	leche
wine	jugo
coffee	batido
juice	café
milk	vino

Clothing	La ropa
shorts	camisa
jacket	medias
hat	calzoncillos
shirt	pantalones
stockings	sombrero
raincoat	guantes
belt	falda
gloves	impermeable
skirt	cinturón
pants	chaqueta

Connect each word with its correct translation.

Shopping	Las compras
bill	ganga
discount	venta
sale	cuenta
price	descuento
bargain	precio

Commands	Mandatos
Speak!	¡Cállese!
Go!	¡Coma!
Shut up!	¡Escriba!
Write!	¡Vaya!
Come!	¡Hable!
Eat!	¡Espere!
Wake up!	¡Siéntese!
Sit down!	¡Despiértese!
Wait!	¡Escuche!
Listen!	¡Venga!

Verbs	Los verbos
open	llorar
cry	vender
carry	abrir
sell	viajar
travel	llevar

More verbs	Más verbos
save	gritar
rest	salir
wish	ahorrar
arrive	traducir
leave	buscar
break	descansar
enjoy	disfrutar
yell	quebrar
translate	desear
look for	llegar

Connect each word with its correct translation.

When?	¿Cuándo?
yesterday	ayer
before	ahorita
tomorrow	a veces
right now	antes
sometimes	mañana

Where?	¿Dónde?
outside	hacia
far	arriba
up	afuera
down	lejos
towards	abajo

Sports	Los deportes
team	estadio
coach	partido
stadium	equipo
practice	entrenador
match	práctica

Toys	Los juguetes
blocks	dron
skates	rompecabezas
ball	cubos
drone	pelota
puzzle	patines

Things	Objetos
pin	desodorante
lock	cepillo
box	alfiler
deodorant	carta
magazine	caja
letter	cerradura
tape	revista
comb	cinta
brush	peine

APPENDIX A

Basic Verb Tenses

Present Indicative: *Todos los días . . .* (Every day . . .)

This is what happens when we refer to "every day" actions in the present tense. Instead of adding *-ndo* endings, the words shift to <u>the one who completes the action</u>. More importantly, the forms of **estar** are dropped. This next pattern is the same for most verbs in Spanish, called the REGULARS. Watch:

<u>to speak</u>	***hablar***
I speak	***hablo***
you speak; he, she speaks	***habla***
you (plural), they speak	***hablan***
we speak	***hablamos***

<u>to eat</u>	<u>***comer***</u>
I eat	***como***
you eat; he, she eats	***come***
you (plural), they eat	***comen***
we eat	***comemos***

<u>to write</u>	<u>***escribir***</u>
I write	***escribo***
you write; he, she writes	***escribe***
you (plural), they write	***escriben***
we write	***escribimos***

See? These three endings send a signal as to who's involved in the action:

Yo	____***o***
Ellos, Ellas, Ustedes	____***n***
Nosotros	____***mos***

 **QUICK TIPS**

- Notice how the *-ar* endings differ from those in the *-er* and *-ir* verbs, yet all the forms seem to follow a similar pattern. This information will be helpful as you pick up more action forms later on.
- Again, there's no need to put the subject pronouns in front of these verb forms since most of the endings tell the listener who's doing the action.
- Look at what happens to the ***nosotros*** form of *-ir* verbs. It keeps the "*i*" to make ***imos***. Here's a little jingle to help you recall Present Tense *-ir* verb conjugations: "IT'S JUST LIKE THE ***ER***, BUT WITH ***IMOS*** AT THE END!"
- As always, the ***tú*** forms of verb conjugations can be acquired at a later time. Learning these four forms is really all you need, and will make memorization a whole lot easier!
- This third form can also refer to "*it*":   It eats a lot! *¡Come mucho!*
- Here's how the negative and question forms are put together:
  Does he live in the house?   *¿Vive en la casa?*
  No, he doesn't live in the house.   *No, no vive en la casa.*
- Sometimes this present indicative tense can be translated differently into English. For example:
  Siempre hablo español.   I always speak Spanish.
  I always do speak Spanish.
  I'm always speaking Spanish.
- A great way to remember verb patterns is to write down all four forms on one side of a 3x5 card, and then put the verb infinitive in large letters on the other side. Separate by color if you feel inclined, and then use them as flashcards! Simply look at the infinitive and try to recall each of its conjugated forms without turning the card over. Develop ways to keep things simple:

hablo	*como*	*escribo*
habla(n)	*come(n)*	*escribe(n)*
hablamos	*comemos*	*escribimos*

Los irregulares (The Irregular Ones)

In the present tense, regular verbs were easy to work with because they all followed very simple patterns. Irregular verbs differ however, and must be divided into groups which share similar characteristics. One of the largest groups of irregular verbs are called the radical "stem-changers." Here are two of its largest families:

The "*ie*" Family

In one family of verbs, the letter "*e*" (stem) inside the word changes to "*ie*." As you read through these next irregular forms, put emphasis on the "*ie*" sound. Fortunately, the rest of the letters are the same as regular verbs in the present tense. And look at the **nosotros** form - it doesn't even change at all!

**entender**	<u>to understand</u>
**entiendo**	I understand
**entiende**	you understand; he, she understands
**entienden**	you (plural), they understand
**entendemos**	we understand
**querer**	<u>to want</u>
**quiero**	I want
**quiere**	you want; he, she wants
**quieren**	you (plural), they want
**queremos**	we want
**perder**	<u>to lose</u>
**pierdo**	I lose
**pierde**	you lose; he, she loses
**pierden**	you (plural), they lose
**perdemos**	we lose

Now read a few examples:

I understand a lot of Spanish.	_**Entiendo mucho español.**_
John wants more money.	_**Juan quiere más dinero.**_
They always lose their books.	_**Siempre pierden sus libros.**_

If you need more, search "present indicative stem-changers" and memorize the words you need!

The "*ue*" Family

Just down the road from the "*ie*" family is a similar group of Spanish verbs that also have a stem-change in the middle. They're the "*ue*" family and must be memorized, just like their cousins up the street. The forms below hold true for most "*ue*" verbs in the present tense, so pay special attention to what's going on. This time, the "*o*" changes to "*ue*." Again, the *nosotros* form is regular. These three are just examples:

contar	to count
cuento	I count
cuenta	you count; he, she counts
cuentan	you (plural), they count
contamos	we count
poder	to be able to (can)
puedo	I can
puede	you, he, she can
pueden	you (plural), they can
podemos	we can
dormir	to sleep
duermo	I sleep
duerme	you sleep; he, she sleeps
duermen	you (plural), they sleep
dormimos	we sleep

Examples:

We count the books every day.	*Contamos los libros cada día.*
I can write in Spanish.	*Puedo escribir en español.*
She sleeps in her bed.	*Ella duerme en su cama.*

The "*e*" to "*i*" Bunch

Watch out! Some "changing" verbs are slightly different, because their "stem" shifts from an "*e*" to an "*i*." Here's a typical example. You should know by now what these four forms mean:

pedir   (to ask for)

pido	*Pido más dinero.*	I ask for more money.
pide	*No pide nada.*	She doesn't ask for anything.
piden	*Piden muchas cosas.*	They ask for lots of things.
pedimos	*Pedimos un Uber.*	We ask for an Uber.

Now it's your turn. Review the above examples as you write your own sentences below. Keep in mind that each action takes place in the present time:

medir   (to measure)

mido	*Siempre mido el agua.*	(I always meaure the water.)
mide	_____	
miden	_____	
medimos	_____	

Are you adding the following phrases to the end of each line? Remember – we're still on Planet Present Tense!:

todos los días	*Pierden muchos papeles todos los días.*
cada semana	*Cada semana cuento el dinero.*
siempre	*Siempre medimos la fruta.*
nunca	*Nunca duermo en el sofá.*
a veces	*Los niños quieren la leche a veces.*

Los verbos viciosos (Vicious Verbs)

It's time to take on the other "misfit" verbs that seem to follow no rules at all. To make it easier, study each of the following separately. This is one you may already know:

ir	to go
voy	I go
va	you go; he, she goes
van	you (plural), they go
vamos	we go

Try filling in these translations all by yourself:

tener	to have
tengo	_____
tiene	_____
tienen	_____
tenemos	_____

estar	to be	*ser*	to be
estoy	_____	*soy*	_____
está	_____	*es*	_____
están	_____	*son*	_____
estamos	_____	*somos*	_____

Talk about "irregular"! Check these out:

venir (to come)	*decir* (to say)	*oír* (to hear)
vengo	*digo*	*oigo*
viene	*dice*	*oye*
vienen	*dicen*	*oyen*
venimos	*decimos*	*oímos*

Now, practice reading aloud:

¿Cuándo vienen los doctores?

¿Qué dice usted?

¿Quién oye la música?

This next set has a "*go*" in the *yo* form. They're called the "*YO-GO'S*"! Notice the "shortcut" to memorization – simply add an "*n*" to indicate the plural:

hacer (to do, make)   *poner* (to put)

hago   *pongo*

hace(n)   *pone(n)*

hacemos   *ponemos*

salir (to leave)   *traer* (to bring)

salgo   *traigo*

sale(n)   *trae(n)*

salimos   *traemos*

caer (to fall)
caigo
cae(n)
caemos

Español: *Traigo mi libro, hago mucho trabajo y salgo a las cinco.*

English: _____

Learning irregular present tense verbs is a lifelong process and one of the biggest hurdles for every Spanish student! So, get started on them today!

Keep looking for "irregular verbs" in Spanish online, but don't overdo it. Only practice the ones you'll use!

caber (to fit)   *ver* (to see)   *dar* (to give)

quepo   *veo*   *doy*

cabe (n)   *ve (n)*   *da (n)*

cabemos   *vemos*   *damos*

Now, study:

El piano no cabe en la casa.

Siempre vemos a nuestros amigos.

Ellas dan dinero.

QUICK TIPS

- The informal **tú** forms for most verbs are formed by adding an "**s**" to the "he, she, you" form (i.e. ***Ella sabe. Tú sabes.***).
- In Spanish, the little word "***a***" must be used when an action is directed toward people. It's called the personal "***a***." Notice its position:

We always visit Mary.	***Siempre visitamos a María.***
I don't understand the teacher.	***No entiendo a la profesora.***
Can you call your friend?	***¿Puede usted llamar a su amigo?***

- A few other verbs cause trouble, too, like those ending in the letters "***uir***" that have the "***y***" sound. Read these examples aloud:

incluir (to include)

incluyo, incluye(n), incluimos	***El libro incluye un diccionario.***

contribuir (to contribute)

contribuyo, contribuye(n), contribuimos	***Ellos contribuyen mucho.***

- Or, those ending in either "***cer***" or "***cir***," since they also change in the ***yo*** form:

obedecer (to obey)

obedezco, obedece(n), obedecemos	***No obedezco al profesor.***

traducir (to translate)

traduzco, traduce(n), traducimos	***Siempre traduzco al español.***

Future Indicative:
Mañana . . .
(Tomorrow . . .)

Believe it or not, to talk about the future in Spanish, there are very few changes made to the base verb forms. Generally, all you do is add a few letters at the end. However, you'll need to exaggerate the final accented syllable:

<u>to speak</u>	***hablar***
I'll speak	***hablaré***
you'll, he'll, she'll speak	***hablará***
you'll (pl.), they'll speak	***hablarán***
we'll speak	***hablaremos***

<u>to eat</u>	***comer***
I'll eat	***comeré***
you'll, he'll, she'll eat	***comerá***
you'll (pl.), they'll eat	***comerán***
we'll eat	***comeremos***

 Don't confuse this future "tense" with the other one: ***Voy a ir*** (I'm going to go) is not ***Iré*** (I will go).

<u>to write</u>	***escribir***
I'll write	***escribiré***
you'll, he'll, she'll write	***escribirá***
you'll (pl.), they'll write	***escribirán***
we'll write	***escribiremos***

Now, using this same formula, give it a try with these:

trabajar   ***vender***

_____   _____
_____   _____
_____   _____
_____   _____

Los irregulares (The Irregular Ones)

The following "irregulars" are easy to recall, since they follow a similar pattern. Go ahead and give 'em a try.

tener (to have)	***tendré, tendrá, tendrán, tendremos***
	Tendré una fiesta. I'll have a party.
poner (to put)	***pondré, pondrá, pondrán, pondremos***
venir (to come)	***vendré, vendrá, vendrán, vendremos***
salir (to leave)	***saldré, saldrá, saldrán, saldremos***
poder (to be able to)	***podré, podrá, podrán, podremos***
saber (to know)	***sabré, sabrá, sabrán, sabremos***
querer (to want)	***querré, querrá, querrán, querremos***
hacer (to do, make)	***haré, hará, harán, haremos***
decir (to say, tell)	***diré, dirá, dirán, diremos***

Oh, sure, there are more irregular verbs in Spanish, but these obviously need to be fooled around with first!

QUICK TIPS

- The conditional tense in Spanish is similar to the future tense. It is used to talk about "what would happen" next. See how letters are added at the end of the base verbs. As you practice reading the following words, pay attention to the accent marks:

-ar verbs	I, you, he, she would speak	***hablaría***
	you (pl.), they would speak	***hablarían***
	we would speak	***hablaríamos***
-er, -ir verbs	I, you, he, she would eat	***comería***
	you (pl.), they would eat	***comerían***
	we would eat	***comeríamos***

- And guess what? The conditional tense uses the same irregular base form as the future tense. Look!

   tener (to have) ***tendría, tendría, tendrían, tendríamos***   ***Tendría una fiesta.***
   I'd have a party.

The Preterit Tense: *Ayer . . .* (Yesterday . . .)

Spanish has two basic past tenses – the preterit and the imperfect. Sorry, but it's better if you remember their names. The preterit is a little more common, because it refers to actions that were completed in past time. It kind of *reports, narrates, or sums up activities that were completed* in the past. We'll get to the imperfect tense a little later on.

The PRETERIT

For regular *-ar* verbs, change the endings just like the example:

to work	*trabajar*	
I worked	*trabajé*	*Yo trabajé ayer.*
you, he, she worked	*trabajó*	*¿Trabajó Juana el lunes?*
you (pl.), they worked	*trabajaron*	_____
we worked	*trabajamos*	_____

For regular **-er** and **-ir** actions, change the forms to look like these:

to eat	*comer*	
I ate	*comí*	*No comí muchos frijoles.*
you, he, she ate	*comió*	_____
you (pl.), they ate	*comieron*	_____
we ate	*comimos*	_____

to write	*escribir*	
I wrote	*escribí*	_____
you, he, she wrote	*escribió*	_____
you (pl.), they wrote	*escribieron*	_____
we wrote	*escribimos*	_____

The preterit *tú* form is important because it's used all the time. Listen for the *-aste* and *-iste* endings when family and friends start talking:

- You knew I'd mention the **tú** form. It's kinda unique:

You (informal) worked.	*Trabajaste.*	*¿Trabajaste hoy? No, no trabajé.*
You (informal) ate.	*Comiste.*	*¿Qué comiste? Comí una ensalada.*
You (informal) wrote.	*Escribiste.*	_____

 Did you see how the "we" form looks exactly like the one in the present tense!

QUICK TIPS

To remember the preterit, keep things simple. These are the letters you'll need to know:

trabaj ___ -é
ó aron amos
com ___ -í ió
ieron imos
escrib ___ -í
ió ieron imos

Los irregulares (The Irregular Ones)

You should know by now that the key to remembering irregular verbs is to focus on key patterns instead of each individual word. Create a sentence and translate! Use your phone if you need help!

> This tense is the toughest in Spanish, so it will take awhile. Use flashcards in the app to practice.

(to hear) *oír: oí, oyó, oyeron, oímos*
Oímos la música. _____

(to laugh) *reír: reí, rio, rieron, reímos*

(to read) *leer: leí, leyó, leyeron, leímos*

(to believe) *creer: creí, creyó, creyeron, creímos*

(to sleep) *dormir: dormí, durmió, durmieron, dormimos*

(to die) *morir: morí, murió, murieron, morimos*

(to walk) *andar: anduve, anduvo, anduvieron, anduvimos*

(to be) *estar: estuve, estuvo, estuvieron, estuvimos*

Group them any way you like!

(to give) *dar: di, dio, dieron, dimos*

(to know) *saber: supe, supo, supieron, supimos*

(to be able to) *poder: pude, pudo, pudieron, pudimos*

(to come) *venir: vine, vino, vinieron, vinimos*

(to want) *querer: quise, quiso, quisieron, quisimos*

(to do, to make) *hacer: hice, hizo, hicieron, hicimos*

(to say) *decir: dije, dijo, dijeron, dijimos*

WENT (from **IR**) and **WAS** or **WERE** (from **SER**) have the same forms. Go for it! They're fun to say:

I went/I was	*fui*
you, he, she, it went/you were; he, she, it was	*fue*
you (pl.), they went/you (pl.), they were	*fueron*
we went/we were	*fuimos*

These examples will help you out:

I went to my house	*Fui a mi casa.*
I was the person.	*Fui la persona.*
Where did you go?	*¿Adónde fue?*
Who was it?	*¿Quién fue?*
We didn't go late.	*No fuimos tarde.*
We weren't students.	*No fuimos estudiantes.*

QUICK TIPS

- Continue to look for patterns. For example, anything with "*poner*" inside gets treated the same:

(to put)	*poner: puse, puso, pusieron, pusimos*
(to suppose)	*suponer: supuse, supuso, supusieron, supusimos*
(to bring)	*traer: traje, trajo, trajeron, trajimos*
(to attract)	*atraer: atraje, atrajo, atrajeron, atrajimos*
(to have)	*tener: tuve, tuvo, tuvieron, tuvimos*

  You do it: (to contain) **contener:** _____ _____ _____ _____

- Here, the "*e*" becomes an "*i*" in two of the forms. You can look up others later:

(to feel)	*sentir: sentí, sintió, sintieron, sentimos*
(to ask for)	*pedir: pedí, pidió, pidieron, pedimos*
(to serve)	*servir: serví, sirvió, sirvieron, servimos*

- These all end in the letters "*uir*." As you read and write each word, pay attention to the spelling:

(to build)	*construir: construí, construyó, construyeron, construímos*
(to include)	*incluir: incluí, incluyó, incluyeron, incluímos*
(to destroy)	*destruir:* _____ _____ _____ _____

- Members of the "*cir*" series look alike, too! They end in the same letters, and have no accent marks:

(to produce)	*producir: produje, produjo, produjeron, produjimos*
(to reduce)	*reducir:* _____ _____ _____ _____
(to translate)	*traducir:* _____ _____ _____ _____

- A couple of verbs change meaning when you speak in the preterit:

I know.	*Yo sé.*	I found out.	*Yo supe.*
I know him.	*Lo conozco.*	I met him.	*Lo conocí.*
I don't want to.	*No quiero.*	I refused to.	*No quise.*

- Spelling changes happen in the preterit, but don't fret about that now.

The Imperfect Tense: *Hace años . . .* (Years Ago . . .)

Get ready for another way to talk about the past. It's called the imperfect. Unlike the preterit, which expresses a completed action, the imperfect expresses a continued, customary, or repeated action in the past. In other words, it's used to express "what was happening" or "what used to happen" before.

Let's take a look at a simple formula that shows how to create imperfect forms with most action words. To get a feel for its usage, pay extra attention to the English translations.

For regular -**ar** actions, change the endings just like this example. NOTICE HOW THE *yo* FORM AND THE *Usted*, *él*, OR *ella* FORM ARE EXACTLY THE SAME:

to work	*trabajar*	
I was working	*trabajaba*	*Yo trabajaba en Ecuador.*
you were working;		
he, she was working	*trabajaba*	*Ben trabajaba en Colombia.*
you (pl.), they were working	*trabajaban*	
we were working	*trabajábamos*	

And for regular -**er** and -**ir** actions, the endings are formed differently. Unlike the preterit, these actions were never really started and completed:

to eat	*comer*	
I was eating.	*comía*	*Hace años no comía carne.*
you were eating;		
he, she was eating	*comía*	
you (pl.), they were eating	*comían*	
we were eating	*comíamos*	

Fill in the English. You don't need any help:

to write	*escribir*	
_____	*escribía*	*Escribía mucho cuando estaba en la escuela.*
_____	*escribía*	
_____	*escribían*	
_____	*escribíamos*	

Now, learn the imperfect by contrasting it with the preterit. They're slightly different:

Iba ahí en el verano.	He would go there in the summer. (imperfect)
Fue ahí el 5 de mayo.	He went there on May 5th. (preterit)
Era mi maestro.	He used to be my teacher. (imperfect)
Fue mi maestro.	He was my teacher. (preterit)
Veía el campo.	He was seeing the country-side. (imperfect)
Vio el campo.	He saw the countryside. (preterit)

 To use the *tú* form, add an "*s*": *Trabajabas, comías y escribías.* (You were working, eating, and writing.) There are ONLY THREE irregular verbs in the imperfect, so let's get them over with. Notice how I simplified the forms so I never have to translate:
(to go) <u>*ir*</u>: *iba, iba(n), íbamos*
(to be) <u>*ser*</u>: *era, era(n), éramos*
(to see) <u>*ver*</u>: *veía, veía(n), veíamos*

 QUICK TIPS

Here's an easy guide to differentiating between the "preterit" and the "imperfect." You may want to photograph this part with your phone for easy reference:

PRETERIT: It tells what happened and is **specific**:
- It says that an action began.
- It says that an action ended.
- It says that an action was completed within a definite period of time.

IMPERFECT: It tells what was happening or what used to happen and is **not specific**:
- It describes persons or things when the action is "past."
- It describes customary, repeated, or habitual activities in the past.
- It describes an action, scene, or condition that was continuing for an indefinite period of time.

The Perfect Tense: *Muchas Veces . . .* (Many Times . . .)

Before we learn the next verb tense, let's practice with something called a "past participle." Although it sounds quite technical, the past participles of most "**ar**," "**er**," and "**ir**" verbs are easy to form and even easier to use. To form the past participle, follow this simple pattern.

The -**ar** verbs change to -**ado**, while the -**er** and -**ir** verbs change to "**ido**":

(to speak) *hab**lar***	(to sell) *ven**der***	(to serve) *serv**ir***
(spoken) *hab**lado***	(sold) *ven**dido***	(served) *serv**ido***

Now, here's how they can be used as descriptive words:

It's not a spoken language.	*No es una lengua hablada.*
They are sold.	*Están vendidos.*
The food is served.	*La comida está servida.*

Go for it. Create a few past participles without translating:

entender <u>*entendido*</u>	*plantar* _____
lavar <u>*lavado*</u>	*perder* _____
cerrar _____	*cocer* _____
dormir _____	*quebrar* _____
pintar _____	*reparar* _____

The past participle in both English and Spanish is also needed to talk about what *has taken place*. This tense is actually made up of two words: the past participle, which we just learned, and *haber* (to have).

Watch – compare these sentences:

Bailé.	(preterit)	I danced.
Bailaba.	(imperfect)	I used to dance.
Estaba bailando.	(past progressive)	I was dancing.
He bailado.	(present perfect)	I have danced.

This is the formula. First, form the past participle by changing the ending of a verb to -***ado*** or -***ido***:

lavar (to wash)   ***lavado*** (washed)
comer (to eat)   ***comido*** (eaten)

Some past participle forms ending in -**ido** take a written accent:
traer (to bring)
traído (brought)
Han traído el dinero.
oír (to hear)
oído (heard)
Hemos oído la canción.

Second, add these present forms of ***haber*** (meaning "to have," but don't confuse this one with ***tener***):

I have	***he***
you have; he, she has	***ha***
you (pl.), they have	***han***
we have	***hemos***

And then, put the two parts together:

Yo he lavado el carro.	I have washed the car.
No hemos bailado.	We haven't danced.
Paula ha comido.	Paula has eaten.

Can you translate?

Hemos estudiado. _____

No he hablado.   _____

¿Han corrido?   _____

Los irregulares (The Irregular Ones)

As you may have guessed, some irregular verbs break all the rules. Read each sample aloud as you fill in the English. LEARN THEM! They are very common and you'll sound funny if you get one wrong:

escribir (to write)
    escrito (written)   *He escrito el libro.* <u>I've written the book.</u>

ver (to see)
    visto (seen)   *He visto al doctor.* <u>I've seen the doctor.</u>

poner (to put)
    puesto (put)   *He puesto todo en la mesa.* _____

hacer (to do, to make)
    hecho (done, made)   *He hecho el trabajo.* _____

abrir (to open)
    abierto (opened)   *He abierto las ventanas.* _____

decir (to say)
    dicho (said)   *He dicho muchas cosas.* _____

volver (to return)
    vuelto (returned)   *He vuelto temprano.* _____

romper (to break)
    roto (broken)   *He roto la silla.* _____

cubrir (to cover)
    cubierto (covered)   *He cubierto todo.* _____

QUICK TIPS

To share what "had happened" beforehand, learn the past perfect tense:

I, you, she, he, it had
había (hablado)
Julia había hablado antes.

you (pl.), they had
habían (comido)

we had **habíamos (escrito)**

The Hardest Thing to Learn in Spanish

A Few Words About **El subjuntivo** (The Subjunctive Mood). Have you ever experienced feelings of doubt, desire, hope, preference, or emotion? Or have you ever felt like making a suggestion or giving a strong opinion? If you have, and would like to share such feelings in Spanish, you'll have to learn how to use the subjunctive mood. It's called a "mood," rather than a "tense," because it's used to express hypothetical situations and important changes in the speaker's attitude.

There are numerous ways to use the subjunctive, so you'll need to invest plenty of time to become familiar with all of its forms and meanings. WE WILL NOT TEACH IT HERE, simply because it is considered an advanced skill, which means you'll need to know a whole lot of Spanish before you can use it correctly. FYI, here are three of its primary uses:

To remember when to use the subjunctive, many folks apply this WEDDING acronym: **W** – Wish or will; **E** – Emotion; **D** – Doubt; **D** – Denial; **I** – Impersonal expressions; **N** – Negation; **G** – God requests

- First, the subjunctive is used when a situation involves something indefinite, uncertain, or contrary to fact:
  Es posible que no venga.   It's possible that he might not come.

- Second, the subjunctive is used to express hope, desires, and emotions.
  ¡Espero que gane usted!   I hope you win!

- Third, it's used when one person expresses his or her will that someone else do something:
  Sugiere que comamos ahora mismo.   He suggests that we eat now.

You'll get the hang of this once you do a little more research. Practice each of the following examples one at a time, and say everything aloud with plenty of feeling.

I hope to God he can see her today.	*Ojalá que pueda verla hoy.*
They want me to write the letter.	*Quieren que yo escriba la carta.*
I don't allow him to smoke.	*No permito que él fume.*
It's probable that I may finish.	*Es probable que yo termine.*
No one likes to do it.	*A nadie le gusta hacerlo.*
We'll leave whenever you want.	*Saldremos cuando usted quiera.*
We allow him to work in the garage.	*Permitimos que él trabaje en el garaje.*
We'll go if it doesn't rain.	*Iremos si no llueve.*

APPENDIX B

English-Spanish Glossary

Spanish-English Glossary

Vocabulary/*Vocabulario*

Most of the words introduced in **Spanish for the Rest of the Us** can be found in the appendix. However, action word forms such as the "Command Words" and specialty vocabulary such as "Traditional Foods" are not part of the appendix.

El and **la** are given only when you might be uncertain which is required. Words that are the same or are both masculine and feminine are indicated by **el/la**.

For more specific information, consult with a Spanish speaker or refer to a dictionary.

English-Spanish

A

a una, un
a little bit poco
a lot (*many*) muchos
a lot (*much*) mucho
a very little bit poquito
about acerca de
above encima
abuse abuso
account cuenta
action la acción
actress la actriz
address la dirección
afterwards después
again otra vez
against contra
agency agencia
agent agente
ahead adelante
air conditioning el aire acondicionado
airplane el avión
airport aeropuerto
all todo
to allow dejar
almost casi
alone solo
along a lo largo de
already ya
also también
always siempre
American americano
and y
angel el ángel
angry enojado

animal el animal
anniversary aniversario
announcement anuncio
another otra, otro
to answer contestar
ant hormiga
anxious ansioso
any cualquiera
anyone cualquiera persona
anywhere cualquiera parte
apartment apartamento
apple manzana
application la aplicación
appointment cita
April abril
apron el delantal
architect el/la arquitecto
area code código de área
around alrededor de
to arrange arreglar
to arrive llegar
ashtray cenicero
asleep dormido
asphalt asfalto
assistant el asistente
astronaut el/la astronauta
at en
at last por fin
athlete el atleta

to attend asistir
attic el desván
August agosto
aunt tía
auto insurance seguro de auto
auto racing automovilismo
available disponible
avenue avenida
to avoid evitar
awhile raro

B

baby el/la bébé
backward al revés
bag bolsa
bakery panadería
bald calvo
ball bola, pelota
balloon globo
banana plátano
bank banco
bar (*drinking*) cantina
barber shop peluquería
bargain ganga
baseball el béisbol
basement sótano
basic básico
basketball el básquetbol
bathrobe bata de baño
bathroom baño
bathtub tina
battery batería

bay bahía
bear (*animal*) oso
beautiful bello
because porque
to be ser
to be (*location and condition*) estar
bed cama
bedroom dormitorio
bee abeja
beer cerveza
before antes
to begin empezar
behind detrás
bellboy el botones
belt el cinturón
besides además
to bet apostar
between entre
Bible Biblia
bicycle bicicleta
big grande
biking ciclismo
bill cuenta
billion el billón
bird pájaro
birth nacimiento
birthday el cumpleaños
bitter amargo
black negro
blackboard el pizarrón
blame culpa
blanket cobija

bleach el blanqueador
blender licuadora
block (*city*) cuadra
to block obstruir
blond rubio
blouse blusa
blue azul
boat barco
boating paseo en bote
boiled herrido
book libro
bookcase librero
boot bota
border frontera
bored aburrido
boss el jefe
both ambos
bottle botella
bottom fondo
bowling el boliche
box (*containter*) caja
boxing boxeo
boyfriend novio
bracelet el brazalete
brakes frenos
branch rama
brave valiente
bread el pan
to break quebrar
brick ladrillo
bride novia
bridge el puente
briefcase el maletín
briefly brevemente
bright brillante
bring traer
broken roto
brooch el broche
broom escoba
broth caldo
brother hermano
brother-in-law cuñado
brown pardo, café
brush cepillo
bucket el balde
buddy compañero
to build construir
building edificio
bus el autobús
bus stop parada de autobús
bush arbusto
but pero
butter mantequilla

C

cabbage repollo
cab driver el taxista
cabinet el gabinete
cable el cable
cake torta
calendar calendario
camel camello
camera cámara
to camp acampar
campgrounds campamento
can lata
can opener el abrelatas
candy el dulce
cap gorra
capital (*letter*) mayúscula
car carro
car lot el lote de carros
card (*playing*) carta
cardboard el cartón
carpenter carpintero
carrot zanahoria
to carry llevar
cartoon caricatura
cashier cajero
cat gato
to cast lanzar, tirar
to catch coger
Catholic católico
to celebrate celebrar
cement cemento
cemetery cementerio
centimeters centímetros
Cantral America Centroamérica
certain cierto
chain cadena
chair silla
chalk tiza
championship campeonato
change cambio
chapter capítulo
charger (*computer*) cargadora
to chart platicar
check el cheque
to check revisar
checkers juego de damas
cheese queso
chef cocinero
cherry cereza

chess el ajedrez
chicken pollo
child niña, niño
chimney chimenea
China China
Christian cristiano
Christmas la Navidad
church iglesia
cigarette cigarrillo
circus circo
clarinet el clarinete
clean limpio
clever listo
client el cliente
climate clima, tiempo
climate change cambio climático
to climb subir
clock el reloj
to close cerrar
closed cerrado
closet ropero
cloth tela
clothing ropa
cloud la nube
clown payaso
coach el entrenador
coast costa
cockroach cucaracha
coffee el café
coffeemaker cafetera
coin moneda
cold frío
to collect coleccionar
comb el peine
to comb one's hair peinarse
command mandato
communism comunismo
community la comunidad
computer computadora
concert concierto
conditioner (*air*) el acondicionador
conference conferencia
congratulations felicitaciones
contract contrato
to control controlar
conversation la conversación
cook cocinar
cooked cocido
cookie galleta
copier copiadora

corn el maíz
corner esquina
correct correcto
correctly correctamente
couch sofá
countryside campo
couple pareja, par
coupon el cupón
court (*sport*) cancha
court la corte
to court someone pretender
cousin primo
cow vaca
coward el cobarde
crab cangrejo
crazy loco
cream crema
credit card tarjeta de crédito
crime el crimen
cross la cruz
to cry llorar
Cuba Cuba
cup taza
curtain cortina
customs aduana
to cut cortar
cute chulo

D

daily diario
dance el baile
to dance bailar
dangerous peligroso
dark oscuro
dark-haired moreno
darling querido
date fecha
daughter hija
daughter-in-law nuera
dawn madrugada
day el día
day before yesterday anteayer
dead muerto
death la muerte
debit débito
deer venado
degrees grados
democracy democracia
dentist el dentista
deodorant el desodorante

description la descripción
desert desierto
desk escritorio
dessert el postre
detergent el detergente
detour la desviación
to develop desarrollar
devil diablo
dialogue diálogo
diamond el diamante
dictionary diccionario
diet dieta
diffferent diferente
difficult difícil
dining room el comedor
dirt tierra
dirty sucio
discount descuento
to discuss discutir
dish el traste
distance distancia
to do hacer
doctor el/la médico
dog perro
doll muñeca
dollar el dólar
domestic doméstico
door puerta
doorbell el timbre
dot punto
doubt duda
down payment el enganche
downtown centro
downward abajo
to draw dibujar
drawer el cajón
to dream soñar
dress vestido
dresser el tocador
drink bebida
to drink beber, tomar
driver's license licencia de chofer
drug droga
drum el tambor
dry seco
dryer secadora
duck pato
dumb tonto
during mientras
dusk el anochecer
dust polvo

E

each cada
early temprano
ear buds los audífonos
earring el arete
east este
easy fácil
easy chair el sillón
effectively efectivamente
egg huevo
eight ocho
eighteen diez y ocho
eighty ochenta
election elección
electric eléctrico
electricity la electricidad
elegant elegante
elephant el elefante
elevator el elevador
eleven once
emergency emergencia
employee empleado
empty vacío
end el fin
enemy enemigo
engine el motor
engineer ingeniero
England Inglaterra
English inglés
to enjoy oneself divertirse
enough bastante
entrance entrada
envelope el sobre
event evento
every day todos los días
everybody todos, todo el mundo
everywhere por todas partes
example ejemplo
excellent excelente
exercise ejercicio
exit salida
to exit salir
expensive caro
experience experiencia

F

factory fábrica
faith la fe
faithful fiel
fall (season) otoño
family familia
famous famoso

fan fanático
fantastic fantástico
far lejos
farm finca
farmer campesino
fat gordo
father el padre
father-in-law suegro
fault falta, culpa
favorite favorito
fear miedo
feather pluma
February febrero
Fence cera
few pocos
fiancé novio
field campo
fifteen quince
fifty cincuenta
fight pleito
finally finalmente, por fin
to find encontrar
to finish terminar
fireman bombero
fireworks fuegos artificiales
first primer, primero
fish el pez
fish (cooked) pescado
to fish pescar
fisherman el pescador
five cinco
five hundred quinientos
to fix reparar
flag bandera
flavor el sabor
to float flotar
floor piso
floor tile baldosa
flower la flor
fly (insect) mosca
to fly volar
fog neblina
following siguiente
food comida
for para, por
for rent se alquila
for sale se vende
forest el bosque
to forget olvidar
fork el tenedor
form forma
forward adelante
four cuarto
fourteen catorce

forty cuarenta
France Francia
fresh fresco
Friday viernes
fried frito
friend amigo
friendly amistoso
from desde, de
frown ceño
frying pan la sartén
full lleno
fun la diversión
funny chistoso
furious furioso
furniture los muebles
furniture store mueblería

G

game juego
gang pandilla
garage el garaje
garden el jardín
gardener el jardinero
gardening jardinería
garlic ajo
gas station gasolinera
gate el portón
to get dressed vestirse
ghost el fantasma
giraffe jirafa
girlfriend novia
to give dar
glass vidrio
glass (drinking) vaso
glove el guante
goat chivo
God Dios
gold oro
good bueno
good-bye adiós
government gobierno
grammar gramática
grams gramos
grandchild nieta, nieto
grandfather abuelo
grandmother abuela
grape uva
grapefruit toronja
grass pasto, hierba
gray gris
green verde
green bean judía verde
groom novio
guide el/la guía

to guess adivinar
guitar guitarra
gum el chicle
gymnasium gimnasio

H

haircut el corte de pelo
half la mitad, medio
hallway pasillo
ham el jamón
hamburger
  hamburguesa
hammer martillo
hand la mano
handkerchief pañuelo
handsome guapo
hanger gancho
to happen suceder,
  pasar
hard (*to touch*) duro
hat sombrero
to hate odiar
to have tener
he él
health la salud
heart el corazón
heat el calor
heating la calefacción
heaven cielo
height estatura
helicopter helicóptero
hell infierno
hello hola
helper el/la ayudante
her ella, su
here acá, aquí
hers suyo, suya
highway carretera
hill cerro
him él
hippopotamus
  hipopótamo
his su, suyo, suya
Hispanic hispánico,
  hispano
to hit golpear, pegar
holy santo
homework tarea
honest honesto
honey la miel
hope esperanza
horse caballo
horseback riding
  montar a caballo
hose manguera

hospital el hospital
hot caliente
hot (*spicy*) picante
hot dog perro
  caliente
house casa
How many? ¿Cuántos?
How much? ¿Cuánto?
however sin embargo
hug abrazo
hundred cien
hundreds cientos
hunger el hambre
hunting caza
husband esposo

I

I yo
ice hielo
ice cream helado
if si
immediately
  inmediatamente
to import importar
importance importancia
important importante
in en
in front of enfrente de
inches pulgadas
incorrect incorrecto
inexpensive barato
information la
  información
insect insecto
inside adentro
instrument instrumento
intelligent inteligente
interesting interesante
interview entrevista
introduction la
  introducción, la
  presentación
iron plancha
island isla

J

jacket chaqueta
jail la cárcel
January enero
Japan el Japón
jar frasco
jealous celoso
Jesus Christ Jesucristo
Jew judío

jewel joya
jewelry shop joyería
job trabajo
to join juntar
joke el chiste
juice jugo
July julio
June junio
jungle selva
just apenas
justice justicia

K

key la llave
kilogram (*2.2 pounds*)
  kilogramo
**kilometer (*5/8 of a
  mile*)** kilómetro
king el rey
kiss beso
to kiss besar
kitchen cocina
kite el cometa
knapsack mochila
knife cuchillo
knot nudo

L

ladder escalera
lady dama, señora
lake lago
lamp lámpara
language el idioma,
  lengua
laptop la portátil
large grande
last último
last night anoche
late tarde
later luego
Latin latino
laughter risa
laundromat lavandería
law la ley
lawyer abogado
lazy perezoso
leaf hoja
to learn aprender
to leave salir
to leave behind
  dejar
left (*direction*)
  izquierda
lemon el limón

lemonade limonada
to lend prestar
length longitud
less menos
lesson la lección
letter (*alphabet*) letra
letter (*mail*) carta
lettuce lechuga
library biblioteca
license plate placa
lie (*not true*) mentira
to lie down acostarse
life vida
light la luz
light (*not dark*) claro
likewise igualmente
lion el león
list lista
to listen escuchar
liter litro
living room sala
lobster langosta
lock cerradura
long largo
to look for buscar
to lose perder
lost perdido
love el amor
to love amar
lovely hermoso
lover el amante
low bajo
lowercase (*letter*)
  minúscula
luck la suerte

M

magazine revista
magic magia
magnificent magnífico
maid criada
mail correo
majority mayoría
to make hacer
to make a call
  hacer una llamada
makeup el maquillaje
mall centro commercial
man el hombre
manager el gerente
manner manera
map mapa
marble (*toy*) canica
March marzo
marriage matrimonio

marvelous maravilloso
match fósforo
maximum máximo
May mayo
meal comida
mean cruel
meaning significado
meat la carne
meat market carnicería
mechanic mecánico
medicine medicina
medium mediano
meeting junta
member miembro
message recado
meter metro
method método
Mexico México
microwave el
    microondas
middle medio
midnight la medianoche
miles millas
milk la leche
milkshake batido de
    leche
million el millón
millionaire millonario
mine mío
minority minoría
minute minuto
miracle milagro
mirror espejo
Miss señorita
to miss faltar
mister el señor
modern moderno
moment momento
Monday lunes
money dinero
monkey mono
month el mes
mop el trapeador
more más
mother la madre
motorcycle motocicleta
mouse el ratón
movie el cine
Mr. sr. (*abr. for* señor)
Mrs. sra. (*abr. for* señora)
mud lodo
museum museo
music música
musician músico
mustard mostaza
my mi, mis

N

nail clavo
name el nombre
napkin servilleta
narrow estrecho
nation la nación
nationality la
    nacionalidad
nature naturaleza
near cerca
necessary necesario
necklace el collar
needle aguja
neighborhood barrio
neither tampoco
nervous nervioso
net la red
never nunca
nevertheless sin
    embargo
news las noticias
newspaper periódico
next próximo, siguiente
nice simpático
nightmare pesadilla
nine nueve
nine hundred
    novecientos
nineteen diez y nueve
ninety noventa
no one nadie
none ninguna, ninguno
noon el mediodía
North America
    Norteamérica
notations apuntes
note nota
notebook cuaderno
nothing nada
notice la notificación
November noviembre
nowadays ahora
nowhere por ningún
    lado
number número
nurse enfermera
nut (*food*) la nuez

O

obesity la obesidad
obvious obvio
ocean océano
October octubre
of de
of the del

offer oferta
office oficina
oil el aceite
old viejo
older mayor
on en
once una vez
one uno
onion cebolla
only sólo
open abierto
operation la operación
opposite contrario
or o
orange (*fruit*) naranja
orange (*color*)
    anaranjado
to order ordenar
our nuestra(s),
    nuestro(s)
out of order
    descompuesto
outlet el enchufe
outside afuera
outskirts las afueras
over sobre
over there allá
overcoat abrigo
owner dueño

P

page página
pain el dolor
paint pintura
painter el pintor
pair par, pareja
pajamas piyama
pants los pantalones
paper el papel
parents los padres
park el parque
to park estacionar
parking
    estacionamiento
party fiesta
to pass pasar
passionate apasionado
passport el pasaporte
past pasado
to pay pagar
payment pago
pea el guisante
peace la paz
pearl perla
pen pluma

pencil el lápiz
people la gente
pepper pimienta
perfectly
    perfectamente
perfume el perfume
person persona
pharmacy farmacia
philosophy filosofía
phone number
    número de teléfono
photo la foto
photography fotografía
pictures los cuardos
pie el pastel
pig puerco
pillow almohada
pin el alfiler
to pitch lanzar
pitcher cántaro
place el lugar, sitio
plant planta
to plant plantar
plastic plástico
plate plato
to play (*a game*) jugar
**to play (*an
    instrument*)** tocar
playground patio de
    recreo
pleasant agradable
please por favor
pliers los alicates
plumber plomero
plumbing tubería
point punta
police policía
policy póliza
political party partido
politics política
pollution la
    contaminación
poor pobre
port cerdo
possession la posesión
possible posible
post office (oficina de)
    correo
postcard tarjeta postal
pot olla
potato papa, patata
pounds libras
poverty pobreza
practice práctica
precious precioso
pregnant embarazada

presentation la presentación
president el presidente
pretty bonito
price precio
printer impresora
problem el problema
product producto
professional profesional
program programa
promise promesa
pronunciation la pronunciación
proud orgulloso
public público
to pull jalar
punishment castigo
purple morado
purse bolsa
to push empujar
to put poner
puzzle el rompecabezas

Q

queen reina
question pregunta
quick rápido
quickly rápidamente
to quit renunciar

R

racket raqueta
rain lluvia
raincoat el impermeable
to raise oneself up levantarse
rake rastrillo
ranch rancho
rat rata
raw crudo
razor navaja
to read leer
reading lectura
ready listo
reason la razón
receipt recibo
to receive recibir
recipe receta
recreation recreo
red rojo
red-headed pelirrojo
refreshment refresco
refrigerator el refrigerador

relative el pariente
religion la religión
repair la reparación
reservation la reservación
respect respeto
to rest descansar
restaurant el restaurante
restroom sanitario
to return volver
review repaso
rhincoeros el rinoceronte
ribbon cinta
rice el arroz
rich rico
to ride (*on the back of an animal*) montar
right (*direction*) derecha
right now ahora mismo
ring anillo
ripe maduro
river río
road camino
road sign la señal
robbery robo
rock roca
rocket el cohete
romantic romántico
room la habitación
rotten podrido
rough áspero
rubber goma
rug alfombra
to run correr

S

sail navegar
saint santo
salad ensalada
salary sueldo
sale venta
salesperson el vendedor, vendedora
salt la sal
salty salado
salvation la salvación
same mismo
same to you igualmente
sand arena
sangria sangría
Saturday sábado
sauce salsa
sausage salchicha

to save (*keep*) ahorrar
saw serrucho
saxophone saxófono, el saxofón
to say decir
scarf bufanda
schedule horario
school escuela
scissors las tijeras
scooter trotineta
screen pantalla
screw tornillo
screwdriver el destornillador
scuba diving buceo
sea el/la mar
season la estación
second segundo
secretary secretario
seed semilla
seesaw el sube y baja
to sell vender
sentence la frase
September septiembre
seven siete
seven hundred setecientos
seventeen diez y siete
seventy setenta
several varios
sex sexo
shampoo el champú
she ella
sheep oveja
sheet (*bed*) sábana
sheet (*paper*) hoja
shirt camisa
shoe zapato
shoe store zapatería
short (*in height*) bajo
short (*in length*) corto
shorts los calzoncillos
shovel pala
to show mostrar
shower ducha
shrimp el camarón
shy tímido
sickness la enfermedad
side lado
sidewalk acera
signal light semáforo
silver plata
sincere sincero
sincerely sinceramente
to sing cantar
single soltero

sister hermana
sister-in-law cuñada
to sit down sentarse
site sitio, el lugar
six seis
sixteen diez y seis
sixty sesenta
size tamaño
to skate patinar
skates los patines
ski esquiar
skill la habilidad
skirt falda
skyscraper el rascacielos
to sleep dormir
slippers las pantuflas
slow lento
slowly despacio
small chico
smile sonrisa
smoke humo
to smoke fumar
smooth suave
snake víbora
snow la nieva
so tan
soap el jabón
soccer el fútbol
social security seguro social
socks los calcetines
soft blando
soldier soldado
some algún, algunos, algunas; uno(s), una(s)
someone alguien
sometimes a veces
somewhere por algún lugar
son hijo
son-in-law yerno
soon pronto
soul el alma
sound sonido
soup sopa
sour agrio
South America Sudamérica
Spain España
Spanish español
to speak hablar
special especial
spend gastar
spider araña
spoon cuchara

sport el deporte
sports coat saco
spring primavera
stadium estadio
stain mancha
stairs las escaleras
stamp sello
station la estación
steak el bistec
step paso
stereo estéreo
stick palo
to stick pegar, adherir
still aún
stone piedra
store tienda
stove estufa
strange estraño
strawberry fresa
street la calle
strike huelga
strong fuerte
structure estructura
student el estudiante
studious aplicado
study estudio
stupid estúpido
subway metro (*abr. for* metropolitano)
suddenly de repente
sugar el/la azúcar
suit el traje
suitcase maleta
summer verano
Sunday domingo
sunset puesta del sol
supermarket supermercado
sure seguro
surname apellido
surgeon cirujano
surprised sorprendido
to survive sobrevivir
sweater el suéter
sweatsuit el traje de entrenamiento
sweet dulce
sweethearts los novios
to swim nadar
swimming pool piscina
swimsuit el traje de baño
symbol símbolo

T

T-shirt camiseta
table mesa
tablecloth el mantel
to take tomar
to take advantage aprovechar
to take away quitar
tall alto
taxes impuestos
tea el té
teacher maestro
team equipo
tear (*crying*) lágrima
telephone teléfono
television la televisión, el televisor
temperature temperatura
ten diez
tennis el tenis
terrible terrible
terrific terrífico
test el examen
thanks gracias
that que
that (*there*) esa, ese, eso
that (*one*) ésa, ése
the (*f*) la, las
the (*m*) el, los
their su, sus, suyos
theirs suyo
theme el tema
then entonces
there ahí
there is, there are hay
therefore por eso
there estos, estas
these ones éstos, éstas
they ellos, ellas
thief el ladrón
thin flaco
thing cosa
thirst la sed
thirteen trece
thirty treinta
this esto, esta, este
this one ésta, éste
those esos, esas
those (*over there*) aquéllos aquéllas
thousand mil
thread hilo
three tres
throat garganta

to throw tirar
Thursday jueves
ticket boleto
tide marea
tie corbata
tiger el tigre
time (*hour*) hora
time tiempo
tip propina
tire (*auto*) llanta
tired cansado
to a
to the al
toaster tostador
today hoy
together juntos
toilet excusado
tomorrow mañana
tongue lengua, el idioma
too, also también
too much demasiado
tool herramienta
to touch tocar
tourist el/la turista
towards hacia
towel toalla
town pueblo
traffic tráfico
train el tren
training entrenamiento
to translate traducir
trash can el bote de basura
to travel viajar
travel agency agencia de viajes
treasure tesoro
tree el árbol
truck el camión
truck driver camionero
to trust confiar
truth la verdad
to try probar
Tuesday martes
turkey pavo
twelve doce
twenty veinte
twin gemelo
two dos
to type escribir a máquina

U

umbrella el paraguas
underneath debajo

underwear ropa interior
United States Estados Unidos
university la universidad
until hasta
upward arriba
usually usualmente

V

vacation la vacación
vaccine vacuna
vacuum cleaner la aspidora
valley el valle
vase florero
very muy
very few poquitos
very pretty muy lindo
video video
view vista
violence violencia
violent violento
violin el violín
to visit visitar
vocabulary vocabulario
voice la voz
volleyball el vóleibol
vote voto

W

waiter mesero
waitress mesera
to walk caminar
wallet cartera
war guerra
to wash lavar
washbasin lavabo
washer la lavadora
watch el reloj
to watch mirar
water el agua
wave ola
we nosotros, nosotras
weak débil
weapon el arma
weather tiempo, el clima
web site sitio web
wedding boda
Wednesday miércoles
week semana
to weigh pesar
weight peso
welcome bienvenidos
well-mannered educado

What? ¿Qué?
When? ¿Cuándo?
Where? ¿Dónde?, ¿Adónde?
Which? ¿Cuál?
white blanco
Who? ¿Quién?
Why? ¿Por qué?
wide ancho
wife esposa
wild salvaje
window ventana
wine vino
wine and fruit juice sangría
winter invierno

wire el alambre
to wish desear
with con
with me conmigo
with you (*between friends, family*) contigo
with him/her/ them consigo
without sin
woman la mujer
wood madera
word palabra
work trabajo
to work trabajar
world mundo

writer el escritor
written escrito
wrong equivocado

Y

yard patio
year año
yellow amarillo
yes sí
yesterday ayer
to yell gritar
yet todavía, aún
to yield ceder
you (*between friends and family*) tú
you usted

you guys ustedes
young joven
young man el joven
younger menor
your (*between friends and family*) tu
your su
yours suyo
yours (*between friends and family*) tuyo

Z

zebra cebra
zero cero
zip code zona postal
zoo zoológico

Spanish-English

A

a to
a lo largo de along
a veces sometimes
abajo downward
abeja bee
abierto open
abogado lawyer
abrazo hug
el abrelatas can opener
abrigo overcoat
abril April
abuela grandmother
abuelo grandfather
aburrido bored
abuso abuse
acá here
acampar to camp
la acción action
el aceite oil
acera sidewalk
acerca de about
el acondicionador air conditioner
acostarse to lie down
la actriz actress
adelante ahead, forward
además besides
adentro inside
adherir to stick
adiós good-bye
adivinar to guess
¿Adónde? Where?
aduana customs
aeropuerto airport
afuera outside
las afueras outskirts
agencia agency
agencia de viajes travel agency
agente agent
agosto August
agradable pleasant
agrio sour
el agua water
aguja needle
ahí there
ahora nowadays
ahora mismo right now
ahorrar to save (keep)

el aire acondicionado air conditioning
el ajedrez chess
ajo garlic
al to the
al revés backward
el alambre wire
el alfiler pin
alfombra rug
alguien someone
algún, algunos, algunas some
los alicates pliers
allá over there
el alma soul
almohada pillow
alrededor de around
alto tall
el amante lover
amar to love
amargo bitter
amarillo yellow
ambos both
americano American
amigo friend
amistoso friendly
el amor love
anaranjado orange (color)
ancho wide
el ángel angel
anillo ring
el animal animal
aniversario anniversary
año year
anoche last night
el anochecer dusk
ansioso anxious
anteayer day before yesterday
antes before
anuncio announcement
apartamento apartment
apasionado passionate
apellido surname
apenas just
la aplicación application
aplicado studious
apostar to bet
aprender to learn

aprovechar to take advantage
apuntes notations
aquéllos aquéllas those (over there)
aquí here
araña spider
el árbol tree
arbusto bush
arena sand
el arete earring
el arma weapon
el/la arquitecto architect
arreglar to arrange
arriba upward
el arroz rice
asfalto asphalt
el asistente assistant
asistir to attend
áspero rough
la aspidora vacuum cleaner
el/la astronauta astronaut
el atleta athlete
los audífonos ear buds
aún still
el autobús bus
automovilismo auto racing
avenida avenue
el avión airplane
ayer yesterday
el/la ayudante helper
el/la azúcar sugar
azul blue

B

bahía bay
bailar to dance
el baile dance
bajo low; short (in height)
el balde bucket
baldosa floor tile
banco bank
bandera flag
baño bathroom
barato inexpensive

barco boat
barrio neighborhood
básico basic
el básquetbol basketball
bastante enough
bata de baño bathrobe
batería battery
batido de leche milkshake
el/la bébé baby
beber to drink
bebida drink
el béisbol baseball
bello beautiful
besar to kiss
beso kiss
Biblia Bible
biblioteca library
bicicleta bicycle
bienvenidos welcome
el billón billion
el bistec steak
blanco white
blando soft
el blanqueador bleach
blusa blouse
boda wedding
bola ball
boleto ticket
el boliche bowling
bolsa bag, purse
bombero fireman
bonito pretty
el bosque forest
bota boot
el bote de basura trash can
botella bottle
el botones bellboy
boxeo boxing
el brazalete bracelet
brevemente briefly
brillante bright
el broche brooch
buceo scuba diving
bueno good
bufanda scarf
buscar to look for

C

caballo horse
el cable cable
cada each
cadena chain
café brown
el café coffee
cafetera coffeemaker
caja box (*containter*)
cajero cashier
el cajón drawer
los calcetines socks
caldo broth
la calefacción heating
calendario calendar
caliente hot
la calle street
el calor heat
calvo bald
los calzoncillos shorts
cama bed
cámara camera
el camarón shrimp
cambio change
cambio climático
    climate change
camello camel
caminar to walk
camino road
el camión truck
camionero truck driver
camisa shirt
camiseta T-shirt
campamento
    campgrounds
campeonato
    championship
campesino farmer
campo field; countryside
cancha court (*sport*)
cangrejo crab
canica marble (*toy*)
cansado tired
cantar to sing
cántaro pitcher
cantina bar (*drinking*)
capítulo chapter
la cárcel jail
cargadora charger
    (*computer*)
caricatura cartoon
la carne meat
carnicería meat
    market
caro expensive

carpintero carpenter
carretera highway
carro car
carta letter (*mail*);
    card (*playing*)
cartera wallet
el cartón cardboard
casa house
casi almost
castigo punishment
católico Catholic
catorce fourteen
caza hunting
cebolla onion
cebra zebra
ceder to yield
celebrar to celebrate
celoso jealous
cementerio cemetery
cemento cement
cenicero ashtray
ceño frown
centímetros
    centimeters
centro downtown
centro commercial mall
Centroamérica
    Cantral America
cepillo brush
cera Fence
cerca near
cerdo port
cereza cherry
cero zero
cerrado closed
cerradura lock
cerrar to close
cerro hill
cerveza beer
el champú shampoo
chaqueta jacket
el cheque check
el chicle gum
chico small
chimenea chimney
China China
el chiste joke
chistoso funny
chivo goat
chulo cute
ciclismo biking
cielo heaven
cien hundred
cientos hundreds
cierto certain
cigarrillo cigarette

cinco five
cincuenta fifty
el cine movie
cinta ribbon
el cinturón belt
circo circus
cirujano surgeon
cita appointment
el clarinete clarinet
claro light (*not dark*)
clavo nail
el cliente client
clima weather; climate
el cobarde coward
cobija blanket
cocido cooked
cocina kitchen
cocinar cook
cocinero chef
código de área
    area code
coger to catch
el cohete rocket
coleccionar to collect
el collar necklace
el comedor dining room
el cometa kite
comida food, meal
compañero buddy
computadora
    computer
la comunidad
    community
comunismo
    communism
con with
concierto concert
conferencia conference
confiar to trust
conmigo with me
consigo with him/
    her/them
construir to build
la contaminación
    pollution
contestar to answer
contigo with you
    (*between friends,
    family*)
contra against
contrario opposite
contrato contract
controlar to control
la conversación
    conversation
copiadora copier

el corazón heart
corbata tie
correctamente
    correctly
correcto correct
correo mail, post
    office
correr to run
cortar to cut
la corte court
el corte de pelo
    haircut
cortina curtain
corto short (*in length*)
cosa thing
costa coast
crema cream
criada maid
el crimen crime
cristiano Christian
crudo raw
cruel mean
la cruz cross
cuaderno notebook
cuadra block (*city*)
¿Cuál? Which?
cualquiera any
cualquiera parte
    anywhere
cualquiera persona
    anyone
¿Cuándo? When?
¿Cuánto? How much?
¿Cuántos? How many?
los cuardos pictures
cuarenta forty
cuarto four
Cuba Cuba
cucaracha cockroach
cuchara spoon
cuchillo knife
cuenta account
cuenta bill
culpa blame, fault
el cumpleaños
    birthday
cuñada sister-in-law
cuñado brother-in-law
el cupón coupon

D

dama lady
dar to give
de from; of
de repente suddenly

debajo underneath

débil weak

débito debit

decir to say

dejar to leave behind; to allow

del of the

el delantal apron

demasiado too much

democracia democracy

el dentista dentist

el deporte sport

derecha right (*direction*)

desarrollar to develop

descansar to rest

descompuesto out of order

la descripción description

descuento discount

desde from

desear to wish

desierto desert

el desodorante deodorant

despacio slowly

después afterwards

el destornillador screwdriver

el desván attic

la desviación detour

el detergente detergent

detrás behind

el día day

diablo devil

diálogo dialogue

el diamante diamond

diario daily

dibujar to draw

diccionario dictionary

dieta diet

diez ten

diez y nueve nineteen

diez y ocho eighteen

diez y seis sixteen

diez y siete seventeen

diferente diffferent

difícil difficult

dinero money

Dios God

la dirección address

discutir to discuss

disponible available

distancia distance

la diversión fun

divertirse to enjoy oneself

doce twelve

el dólar dollar

el dolor pain

doméstico domestic

domingo Sunday

¿Dónde? Where?

dormido asleep

dormir to sleep

dormitorio bedroom

dos two

droga drug

ducha shower

duda doubt

dueño owner

el dulce candy

dulce sweet

duro hard (*to touch*)

E

edificio building

educado well-mannered

efectivamente effectively

ejemplo example

ejercicio exercise

él he, him

el the (*m*)

elección election

la electricidad electricity

eléctrico electric

el elefante elephant

elegante elegant

el elevador elevator

ella she, her

ellos, ellas they

embarazada pregnant

emergencia emergency

empezar to begin

empleado employee

empujar to push

en at, in, on

el enchufe outlet

encima above

encontrar to find

enemigo enemy

enero January

la enfermedad sickness

enfermera nurse

enfrente de in front of

el enganche down payment

enojado angry

ensalada salad

entonces then

entrada entrance

entre between

el entrenador coach

entrenamiento training

entrevista interview

equipo team

equivocado wrong

ésa, ése that (*one*)

esa, ese, eso that (*there*)

escalera ladder

las escaleras stairs

escoba broom

escribir a máquina to type

escrito written

el escritor writer

escritorio desk

escuchar to listen

escuela school

esos, esas those

España Spain

español Spanish

especial special

espejo mirror

esperanza hope

esposa wife

esposo husband

esquiar ski

esquina corner

ésta, éste this one

la estación season; station

estacionamiento parking

estacionar to park

estadio stadium

Estados Unidos United States

estar to be (*location and condition*)

estatura height

este east

estéreo stereo

esto, esta, este this

estos, estas there

éstos, éstas these ones

estraño strange

estrecho narrow

estructura structure

el estudiante student

estudio study

estufa stove

estúpido stupid

evento event

evitar to avoid

el examen test

excelente excellent

excusado toilet

experiencia experience

F

fábrica factory

fácil easy

falda skirt

falta fault

faltar to miss

familia family

famoso famous

fanático fan

el fantasma ghost

fantástico fantastic

farmacia pharmacy

favorito favorite

la fe faith

febrero February

fecha date

felicitaciones congratulations

fiel faithful

fiesta party

filosofía philosophy

el fin end

finalmente finally

finca farm

flaco thin

la flor flower

florero vase

flotar to float

fondo bottom

forma form

fósforo match

la foto photo

fotografía photography

Francia France

frasco jar

la frase sentence

frenos brakes

fresa strawberry

fresco fresh

frío cold

frito fried

frontera border

fuegos artificiales fireworks

fuerte strong
fumar to smoke
furioso furious
el fútbol soccer

G

el gabinete cabinet
galleta cookie
gancho hanger
ganga bargain
el garaje garage
garganta throat
gasolinera gas station
gastar spend
gato cat
gemelo twin
la gente people
el gerente manager
gimnasio gymnasium
globo balloon
gobierno government
golpear to hit
goma rubber
gordo fat
gorra cap
gracias thanks
grados degrees
gramática grammar
gramos grams
grande big, large
gris gray
gritar to yell
el guante glove
guapo handsome
guerra war
el/la guía guide
el guisante pea
guitarra guitar

H

la habilidad skill
la habitación room
hablar to speak
hacer to do; to make
hacer una llamada
    to make a call
hacia towards
el hambre hunger
hamburguesa
    hamburger
hasta until
hay there is, there are
helado ice cream
helicóptero helicopter

hermana sister
hermano brother
hermoso lovely
herramienta tool
herrido boiled
hielo ice
hierba grass
hija daughter
hijo son
hilo thread
hipopótamo
    hippopotamus
hispánico, hispano
    Hispanic
hoja leaf; sheet (*paper*)
hola hello
el hombre man
honesto honest
hora time (*hour*)
horario schedule
hormiga ant
el hospital hospital
hoy today
huelga strike
huevo egg
humo smoke

I

el idioma language;
    tongue
iglesia church
igualmente likewise,
    same to you
el impermeable raincoat
importancia importance
importante important
importar to import
impresora printer
impuestos taxes
incorrecto incorrect
infierno hell
la información
    information
ingeniero engineer
Inglaterra England
inglés English
inmediatamente
    immediately
insecto insect
instrumento instrument
inteligente intelligent
interesante interesting
la introducción
    introduction
invierno winter

isla island
izquierda left (*direction*)

J

el jabón soap
jalar to pull
el jamón ham
el Japón Japan
el jardín garden
jardinería gardening
el jardinero gardener
el jefe boss
Jesucristo Jesus Christ
jirafa giraffe
joven young
el joven young man
joya jewel
joyería jewelry shop
judía verde green bean
judío Jew
juego game
juego de
    damas checkers
jueves Thursday
jugar to play (*a game*)
jugo juice
julio July
junio June
junta meeting
juntar to join
juntos together
justicia justice

K

kilogramo kilogram
    (*2.2 pounds*)
kilómetro kilometer
    (*5/8 of a mile*)

L

la, las the (*f*)
lado side
ladrillo brick
el ladrón thief
lago lake
lágrima tear (*crying*)
lámpara lamp
langosta lobster
lanzar to pitch, to cast
el lápiz pencil
largo long
lata can
latino Latin
lavabo washbasin

la lavadora washer
lavandería
    laundromat
lavar to wash
la lección lesson
la leche milk
lechuga lettuce
lectura reading
leer to read
lejos far
lengua language;
    tongue
lento slow
el león lion
letra letter (*alphabet*)
levantarse to raise
    oneself up
la ley law
libras pounds
librero bookcase
libro book
licencia de chofer
    driver's license
licuadora blender
el limón lemon
limonada lemonade
limpio clean
lista list
listo ready; clever
litro liter
llanta tire (*auto*)
la llave key
llegar to arrive
lleno full
llevar to carry
llorar to cry
lluvia rain
loco crazy
lodo mud
longitud length
los the (*m pl*)
el lote de carros
    car lot
luego later
el lugar place, site
lunes Monday
la luz light

M

madera wood
la madre mother
madrugada dawn
maduro ripe
maestro teacher
magia magic

magnífico magnificent
el maíz corn
maleta suitcase
el maletín briefcase
mañana tomorrow
mancha stain
mandato command
manera manner
manguera hose
la mano hand
el mantel tablecloth
mantequilla butter
manzana apple
mapa map
el maquillaje makeup
el/la mar sea
maravilloso marvelous
marea tide
martes Tuesday
martillo hammer
marzo March
más more
matrimonio marriage
máximo maximum
mayo May
mayor older
mayoría majority
mayúscula capital
    (*letter*)
mecánico mechanic
mediano medium
la medianoche midnight
medicina medicine
el/la médico doctor
medio half; middle
el mediodía noon
menor younger
menos less
mentira lie (*not true*)
el mes month
mesa table
mesera waitress
mesero waiter
método method
metro meter
**metro (*abr.*
    for metropolitano)**
    subway
México Mexico
mi, mis my
el microondas
    microwave
miedo fear
la miel honey
miembro member
mientras during
miércoles Wednesday

mil thousand
milagro miracle
millas miles
el millón million
millonario millionaire
minoría minority
minúscula lowercase
    (*letter*)
minuto minute
mío mine
mirar to watch
mismo same
la mitad half
mochila knapsack
moderno modern
momento moment
moneda coin
mono monkey
montar to ride (*on the
    back of an animal*)
**montar a
    caballo** horseback
    riding
morado purple
moreno dark-haired
mosca fly (*insect*)
mostaza mustard
mostrar to show
motocicleta motorcycle
el motor engine
mucho a lot (*much*)
muchos a lot (*many*)
mueblería furniture
    store
los muebles furniture
la muerte death
muerto dead
la mujer woman
mundo world
muñeca doll
museo museum
música music
músico musician
muy very
muy lindo very pretty

N

nacimiento birth
la nación nation
la nacionalidad
    nationality
nada nothing
nadar to swim
nadie no one
naranja orange (*fruit*)
naturaleza nature
navaja razor

navegar sail
la Navidad Christmas
neblina fog
necesario necessary
negro black
nervioso nervous
nieta, nieto grandchild
la nieva snow
niña, niño child
ninguna, ninguno none
el nombre name
Norteamérica North
    America
nosotros, nosotras we
nota note
las noticias news
la notificación notice
novecientos nine
    hundred
noventa ninety
novia girlfriend, bride
noviembre November
novio boyfriend, fiancé,
    groom
los novios sweethearts
la nube cloud
nudo knot
nuera daughter-in-law
**nuestra(s),
    nuestro(s)** our
nueve nine
la nuez nut (*food*)
número number
número de teléfono
    phone number
nunca never

O

o or
la obesidad obesity
obstruir to block
obvio obvious
océano ocean
ochenta eighty
ocho eight
octubre October
odiar to hate
oferta offer
oficina office
oficina de correo
    post office
ola wave
olla pot
olvidar to forget
once eleven
la operación
    operation

ordenar to order
orgulloso proud
oro gold
oscuro dark
oso bear (*animal*)
otoño fall (*season*)
otra, otro another
otra vez again
oveja sheep

P

el padre father
los padres parents
pagar to pay
página page
pago payment
pájaro bird
pala shovel
palabra word
palo stick
el pan bread
panadería bakery
pandilla gang
pantalla screen
los pantalones pants
las pantuflas slippers
pañuelo handkerchief
papa potato
el papel paper
par pair, couple
para for
parada de autobús
    bus stop
el paraguas umbrella
pardo brown
pareja pair, couple
el pariente relative
el parque park
partido political party
pasado past
el pasaporte passport
pasar to happen; to
    pass
paseo en bote boating
pasillo hallway
paso step
el pastel pie
pasto grass
patata potato
patinar to skate
los patines skates
patio yard
patio de recreo
    playground
pato duck
pavo turkey
payaso clown

la paz   peace
pegar   to hit; to stick
peinarse   to comb
   one's hair
el peine   comb
peligroso   dangerous
pelirrojo   red-headed
pelota   ball
peluquería   barber
   shop
perder   to lose
perdido   lost
perezoso   lazy
perfectamente   perfectly
el perfume   perfume
periódico   newspaper
perla   pearl
pero   but
perro   dog
perro caliente   hot dog
persona   person
pesadilla   nightmare
pesar   to weigh
pescado   fish (*cooked*)
el pescador   fisherman
pescar   to fish
peso   weight
el pez   fish
picante   hot (*spicy*)
piedra   stone
pimienta   pepper
el pintor   painter
pintura   paint
piscina   swimming pool
piso   floor
piyama   pajamas
el pizarrón   blackboard
placa   license plate
plancha   iron
planta   plant
plantar   to plant
plástico   plastic
plata   silver
plátano   banana
platicar   to chart
plato   plate
pleito   fight
plomero   plumber
pluma   pen; feather
pobre   poor
pobreza   poverty
poco   a little bit
pocos   few
podrido   rotten
policía   police
política   politics
póliza   policy

pollo   chicken
polvo   dust
poner   to put
poquito   a very little bit
poquitos   very few
por   for
por algún
   lugar   somewhere
por eso   therefore
por favor   please
por fin   at last, finally
por ningún
   lado   nowhere
¿Por qué?   Why?
porque   because
por todas
   partes   everywhere
la portátil   laptop
el portón   gate
la posesión   possession
posible   possible
el postre   dessert
práctica   practice
precio   price
precioso   precious
pregunta   question
la presentación
   introduction;
   presentation
el presidente   president
prestar   to lend
pretender   to court
   someone
primavera   spring
primer, primero   first
primo   cousin
probar   to try
el problema   problem
producto   product
profesional   professional
programa   program
promesa   promise
pronto   soon
la pronunciación
   pronunciation
propina   tip
próximo   next
público   public
pueblo   town
el puente   bridge
puerco   pig
puerta   door
puesta del sol   sunset
pulgadas   inches
punta   point
punto   dot

Q

que   that
¿Qué?   What?
quebrar   to break
querido   darling
queso   cheese
¿Quién?   Who?
quince   fifteen
quinientos   five hundred
quitar   to take away

R

rama   branch
rancho   ranch
rápidamente   quickly
rápido   quick
raqueta   racket
raro   awhile
el rascacielos   skyscraper
rastrillo   rake
rata   rat
el ratón   mouse
la razón   reason
recado   message
receta   recipe
recibir   to receive
recibo   receipt
recreo   recreation
la red   net
refresco   refreshment
el refrigerador
   refrigerator
reina   queen
la religión   religion
el reloj   watch, clock
renunciar   to quit
la reparación   repair
reparar   to fix
repaso   review
repollo   cabbage
la reservación
   reservation
respeto   respect
el restaurante   restaurant
revisar   to check
revista   magazine
el rey   king
rico   rich
el rinoceronte
   rhincoeros
río   river
risa   laughter
robo   robbery
roca   rock
rojo   red
romántico   romantic

el rompecabezas
   puzzle
ropa   clothing
ropa interior
   underwear
ropero   closet
roto   broken
rubio   blond

S

sábado   Saturday
sábana   sheet (*bed*)
el sabor   flavor
saco   sports coat
la sal   salt
sala   living room
salado   salty
salchicha   sausage
salida   exit
salir   to leave, to exit
salsa   sauce
la salud   health
la salvación   salvation
salvaje   wild
sangría   sangria, wine
   and fruit juice
sanitario   restroom
santo   saint; holy
la sartén   frying pan
el saxofón, saxófono
   saxophone
se alquila   for rent
se vende   for sale
secadora   dryer
seco   dry
secretario   secretary
la sed   thirst
segundo   second
seguro   sure
seguro de auto   auto
   insurance
seguro social   social
   security
seis   six
sello   stamp
selva   jungle
semáforo   signal light
semana   week
semilla   seed
la señal   road sign
el señor   mister
señora   lady
señorita   Miss
sentarse   to sit down
septiembre   September
ser   to be
serrucho   saw

servilleta napkin
sesenta sixty
setecientos seven hundred
setenta seventy
sexo sex
si if
sí yes
siempre always
siete seven
significado meaning
siguiente next, following
silla chair
el sillón easy chair
símbolo symbol
simpático nice
sin without
sin embargo however, nevertheless
sinceramente sincerely
sincero sincere
sitio place, site
sitio web web site
el sobre envelope
sobre over
sobrevivir to survive
sofá couch
soldado soldier
solo alone
sólo only
soltero single
sombrero hat
soñar to dream
sonido sound
sonrisa smile
sopa soup
sorprendido surprised
sótano basement
sr. (abr. for señor) Mr.
sra. (abr. for señora) Mrs.
su, sus his, her, your, their
suave smooth
el sube y baja seesaw
subir to climb
suceder to happen
sucio dirty
Sudamérica South America
suegro father-in-law
sueldo salary
la suerte luck

el suéter sweater
supermercado supermarket
suyo, suya his, hers, yours, theirs

T

tamaño size
también too, also
el tambor drum
tampoco neither
tan so
tarde late
tarea homework
tarjeta de crédito credit card
tarjeta postal postcard
el taxista cab driver
taza cup
el té tea
tela cloth
teléfono telephone
la televisión television
el televisor television
el tema theme
temperatura temperature
temprano early
el tenedor fork
tener to have
el tenis tennis
terminar to finish
terrible terrible
terrífico terrific
tesoro treasure
tía aunt
tiempo time; weather, climate
tienda store
tierra dirt
el tigre tiger
las tijeras scissors
el timbre doorbell
tímido shy
tina bathtub
tirar to throw, to cast
tiza chalk
toalla towel
el tocador dresser
tocar to touch; to play (an instrument)
todavía yet

todo all
todo el mundo everybody
todos everybody
todos los días every day
tomar to take; to drink
tonto dumb
tornillo screw
toronja grapefruit
torta cake
tostador toaster
trabajar to work
trabajo job, work
traducir to translate
traer bring
tráfico traffic
el traje suit
el traje de baño swimsuit
el traje de entrenamiento sweatsuit
el trapeador mop
el traste dish
trece thirteen
treinta thirty
el tren train
tres three
trotineta scooter
tu your (between friends and family)
tú you (between friends and family)
tubería plumbing
el/la turista tourist
tuyo yours (between friends and family)

U

último last
una vez once
una, un a
unas, unos some
la universidad university
uno one
usted you
ustedes you guys
usualmente usually
uva grape

V

vaca cow
la vacación vacation

vacío empty
vacuna vaccine
valiente brave
el valle valley
varios several
vaso glass (drinking)
veinte twenty
venado deer
el vendedor, vendedora salesperson
vender to sell
venta sale
ventana window
verano summer
la verdad truth
verde green
vestido dress
vestirse to get dressed
viajar to travel
víbora snake
vida life
video video
vidrio glass
viejo old
viernes Friday
vino wine
violencia violence
violento violent
el violín violin
visitar to visit
vista view
vocabulario vocabulary
volar to fly
el vóleibol volleyball
volver to return
voto vote
la voz voice

Y

y and
ya already
yerno son-in-law
yo I

Z

zanahoria carrot
zapatería shoe store
zapato shoe
zona postal zip code
zoológico zoo

English-Spanish Verb Lists

accept, to **aceptar**
add, to **agregar, añadir**
advance, to **avanzar**
advise, to **recomendar**
agree, to **convenir**
allow, to **dejar**
answer, to **contestar**
arrange, to **arreglar**
arrive, to **llegar**
ask for, to **pedir**
ask, to **preguntar**
assist, to **atender**
attend, to **asistir**
avoid, to **evitar**
be, to **ser**
be (*location and
    condition*), to **estar**
be able to, to **poder**
be born, to **nacer**
beg, to **suplicar**
begin, to **comenzar,
    empezar**
believe, to **creer**
belong, to **pertenecer**
bend, to **doblar**
bet, to **apostar**
bite, to **morder**
block, to **obstruir**
boil, to **hervir**
break, to **quebrar,
    romper**
breathe, to **respirar**
bring, to **traer**
build, to **construir**
buy, to **comprar**
call, to **llamar**
camp, to **acampar**
carry, to **llevar**
cast, to **lanzar, tirar**
catch, to **coger**
celebrate, to **celebrar**
change, to **cambiar**
charge, to **cargar**
chart, to **platicar**
check, to **revisar**
choose, to **escoger**
climb, to **subir**
close, to **cerrar**
collect, to **coleccionar**

comb one's hair,
    to **peinarse**
come, to **venir**
confuse, to **confundir**
consider, to **considerar**
contain, to **contener**
control, to **controlar**
convince, to **convencer**
cook, to **cocinar**
correct, to **corregir**
cost, to **costar**
count, to **contar**
court someone,
    to **pretender**
cover, to **cubrir, tapar**
crash, to **chocar**
cross, to **cruzar,
    atravesar**
cry, to **llorar**
cut, to **cortar**
dance, to **bailar**
decide, to **decidir**
desire, to **desear**
destroy, to **destruir**
develop, to **desarrollar**
deliver, to **entregar**
deny, to **negar**
describe, to **describir**
die, to **morir**
dig, to **excavar**
discover, to **descubrir**
discuss, to **discutir**
divide, to **dividir**
do, to **hacer**
draw, to **dibujar**
dream, to **soñar**
drink, to **beber, tomar**
drive, to **manejar**
earn, to **ganar**
eat, to **comer**
empty, to **vaciar**
end, to **acabar, terminar**
enjoy oneself,
    to **divertirse**
enter, to **entrar**
examine, to **examinar**
exit, to **salir**
explain, to **explicar**
fall, to **caer**
fear, to **temer**

feed, to **alimentar**
feel, to **sentir**
fight, to **pelear**
fill, to **llenar**
find, to **encontrar**
find out, to **averiguar**
finish, to **terminar**
fish, to **pescar**
fit, to **caber**
fix, to **reparar**
float, to **flotar**
fly, to **volar**
follow, to **seguir**
forget, to **olvidar**
forgive, to **perdonar**
freeze, to **congelar**
get, to **obtener**
get down, to **bajar**
get dressed, to **vestirse**
get near, to **acercar**
give, to **dar**
go, to **ir**
go out, to **salir**
greet, to **saludar**
grind, to **moler**
grow, to **crecer**
guess, to **adivinar**
hang, to **colgar**
happen, to **suceder,
    pasar**
hate, to **odiar**
have, to **tener**
hear, to **oír**
help, to **ayudar**
hide, to **esconder**
hire, to **contratar**
hit, to **golpear,
    pegar**
hold, to **sostener**
hug, to **abrazar**
hunt, to **cazar**
hurt, to **doler**
imagine, to **imaginar**
import, to **importar**
include, to **incluir**
injure, to **herir**
insert, to **meter**
insist, to **insistir**
install, to **instalar**
interpret, to **interpretar**

invest, to **invertir**
join, to **juntar**
judge, to **juzgar**
jump, to **saltar**
keep, to **guardar**
kick, to **patear**
kiss, to **besar**
know (someone),
    to **conocer**
know (something),
    to **saber**
lay, to **colocar**
lead, to **guiar**
learn, to **aprender**
leave, to **salir**
leave behind, to **dejar**
lend, to **prestar**
let, to **permitir**
lie, to **mentir**
lie down, to **acostarse**
lift, to **levantar**
light, to **encender**
like, to **gustar**
listen, to **escuchar**
live, to **vivir**
look, to **mirar**
look for, to **buscar**
loosen, to **soltar**
lose, to **perder**
love, to **amar**
maintain, to **mantener**
make, to **hacer**
make a call, to **hacer
    una llamada**
mark, to **marcar**
mean, to **significar**
measure, to **medir**
meet, to **encontrar**
miss, to **faltar**
move, to **mover**
need, to **necesitar**
notify, to **notificar**
obey, to **obedecer**
obtain, to **obtener**
offer, to **ofrecer**
open, to **abrir**
oppose, to **oponer**
order, to **ordenar**
owe, to **deber**
park, to **estacionar**

pass, to **pasar**
pay, to **pagar**
permit, to **permitir**
persist, to **persistir**
pick up, to **recoger**
pitch, to **lanzar**
plant, to **plantar**
play (*a game*), to **jugar**
play (*an instrument*),
   to **tocar**
plug in, to **enchufar**
polish, to **bruñir, pulir**
practice, to **practicar**
pray, to **rezar**
prefer, to **preferir**
prepare, to **preparar**
prevent, to **prevenir**
promise, to **prometer**
pronounce,
   to **pronunciar**
protect, to **proteger**
prove, to **probar**
pull, to **jalar**
push, to **empujar**
put, to **poner**
quit, to **renunciar**
rain, to **llover**
raise oneself up,
   to **levantarse**
read, to **leer**
reach, to **alcanzar**
read, to **leer**

receive, to **recibir**
recognize, to **reconocer**
recommend,
   to **recomendar**
reduce, to **reducir**
refer, to **referir**
remember, to **recordar**
rent, to **alquilar**
repair, to **reparar**
repeat, to **repetir**
require, to **requirir**
rest, to **descansar**
retire, to **retirar**
return, to **volver**
ride, to **montar**
run, to **correr**
sail, to **navegar**
save (*keep*), to **ahorrar**
say, to **decir**
scratch, to **buscar**
search, to **buscar**
see, to **ver**
seem, to **parecer**
select, to **seleccionar**
sell, to **vender**
send, to **enviar, mandar**
serve, to **servir**
set, to **colocar**
sew, to **cocer**
shake, to **sacudir**
share, to **compartir**
shoot, to **disparar**

shout, to **gritar**
show, to **mostrar**
sing, to **cantar**
sit down, to **sentarse**
skate, to **patinar**
sleep, to **dormir**
smoke, to **fumar**
snow, to **nevar**
speak, to **hablar**
spend, to **gastar**
stay, to **quedar**
stick, to **pegar, adherir**
stir, to **batir, revolver**
study, to **estudiar**
subtract, to **restar**
sweep, to **barrer**
survive, to **sobrevivir**
swim, to **nadar**
take, to **tomar**
take advantage,
   to **aprovechar**
take away, to **quitar**
take out, to **sacar**
take care of, to **cuidar**
talk, to **hablar**
teach, to **enseñar**
tell, to **decir**
thank, to **agradecer**
think, to **pensar**
threaten, to **amenazar**
throw, to **tirar**
touch, to **tocar**

translate, to **traducir**
travel, to **viajar**
trust, to **confiar**
try, to **probar**
turn around, to **voltear**
turn off, to **apagar**
turn on, to **prender,
   encender**
type, to **escribir a
   máquina**
understand, to
   **comprender,
   entender**
use, to **usar**
visit, to **visitar**
vote, to **votar**
walk, to **caminar,
   andar**
want, to **querer**
wash, to **lavar**
watch, to **mirar**
wear, to **llevar**
weight, to **pesar**
win, to **ganar**
wish, to **desear**
work, to **trabajar**
worry, to **preocupar**
write, to **escribir**
yell, to **gritar**
yield, to **ceder**

The Reflexives

bathe, to **bañarse**
become, to **hacerse**
brush, to **cepillarse**
change address,
   to **mudarse**
comb, to **peinarse**
complain, to **quejarse**
dress, to **vestirse**
fall asleep, to **dormirse**
fall down, to **caerse**

forget about, to **olvidarse**
get angry, to **enojarse**
get better, to **mejorarse**
get sick, to **enfermarse**
get married, to
   casarse
get ready, to **arreglarse**
get up, to **levantarse**
have a good time,
   to **divertirse**

hurry up, to **darse prisa**
leave, to **irse**
lie down, to **acostarse**
make a mistake,
   to **equivocarse**
make fun of, to **burlarse**
put on, to **ponerse**
realize, to **darse
   cuenta de**
remember, to **acordarse**

remove, to **quitarse**
shave, to **afreitarse**
sit down, to **sentarse**
stand up, to **pararse**
stay, to **quedarse**
wake up, to **despertarse**
wash, to **lavarse**
worry about, to
   preocuparse